The Dirt
from
Tripp Street

Everyday lessons about life—
love and loss, sadness and joy,
and all the in-betweens

Daniel S. Wolk

SIMON & SCHUSTER
New York London Toronto Sydney Tokyo Singapore

SIMON & SCHUSTER
Simon & Schuster Building
Rockefeller Center
1230 Avenue of the Americas
New York, New York 10020

SIMON & SCHUSTER and colophon are registered trademarks
of Simon & Schuster Inc.

Designed by Levavi & Levavi
Manufactured in the United States of America

1   3   5   7   9   10   8   6   4   2

Library of Congress Cataloging in Publication Data

Wolk, Daniel S.
The dirt from Tripp Street : everyday lessons about life / Daniel
S. Wolk.
p.   cm.
1. Wolk, Daniel S.   I. Title.
BM755.W58A3   1992
296'.092—dc20
[B]   92-16887
                             CIP

ISBN: 0-671-74771-1

"This Rabbi's a Truck Drivin' Man" and "The Bird Feeder" have previously
appeared in The New York Times (Westchester edition).

To my father, who bequeathed his love of books

To Marion, my friend on Tripp Street

Acknowledgments

I am grateful to friends geographically removed from Tripp Street who made the street come to life: Margery McCabe, assistant, sometimes titler and creator of a jacket concept; Jane Dystel, literary agent, who strengthened my faith with her confidence, skill, and tenacity; Sister Mary Campion SHCJ, whose measuring line has always marked a lovely place for me; Bob Gillette, long-standing friend, long-suffering listener; Dominick Anfuso, who edited this collection of thoughts and granted an opportunity; Cal Whipple, for his experience and insight.

Contents

CONTENTS

Spring

Summer

CONTENTS

Preface

When the English poet William Blake wrote, "To see a world in a grain of sand," I doubt he was referring to the grains of sand deposited near the stone wall of my 1861 farmhouse on Tripp Street. On the other hand, Tripp Street, a meandering road only four-tenths of a mile long as the Jeep jogs and the deer runs, contains more than one grain of truth about the world in which we live. *The Dirt from Tripp Street* reflects on the everyday events and people who pass along Tripp Street.

For instance, there's our ninety-five-year-old matriarch, Mrs. Martha Parsons, with her motto "We Grow Old By Not Growing"; little Jason, who set out to capture the moon and dispel darkness; and Garth, cellular phone and squash racket in hand, who recently completed a major financial merger but didn't find happiness. Why? Doesn't success assure happiness?

Even our dog, a mutt named Teddy of Hopeless Junction, shared a grain of wisdom, asking me to judge a dog by the creature beneath the fur, not by name or social status.

Tripp Street rises for a quarter mile from Heather Place in the south, over Murphy's Hill, then falls back onto Heather Place in the north. Some people say we don't go anywhere, and they may be right. Geographically. But my neighbors have traveled far, dreaming, parenting, aging; losing the way, finding a path. Learning to live with one another and with themselves. And no matter who we are, we spend the hours loving, laughing, crying. So join me on the day I moved into my old farmhouse and discovered God dwelling in a moving van; harvested an apple tree and learned to live each day fully; discovered that technology is not an adequate substitute for human contact.

I cannot guarantee you will "see a world in a grain of sand," but I am certain a brief detour to Tripp Street will provide some down-to-earth thoughts on the spiritual, reflective, and value-oriented aspects of life. As it has for me, a rabbi. Although I continue to explore heavenly and theological spheres (an occupational hazard), I usually return home to Tripp Street for perspective, understanding, and a base from which to wander through the maze of our increasingly complex age. Tripp Street combines the pragmatics of survival near an urban center with the dreams of an escape into meadowlands of the past. Old-timers remember when we were a dirt road, and newcomers rush to make the 7:19 to Grand Central.

City dweller, country resident, and assorted hybrids are welcome to explore Tripp Street, delay over a down-to-earth thought, and perhaps experience a moment of sudden recognition casting the commonplace in a new light. Hopefully you will rise on the rungs of awareness and be touched in a simple yet profound way. And on entering Tripp Street, you may even discover you are very close to home.

Winter

1. Moving Day

◈

Moving Day!

"Welcome to God's Country!" Old Luke's voice climbed Murphy's Hill the day Marion and I moved into our rural farmhouse. "Welcome to God's Country!" How could a clergyman resist moving to "God's Country"? Although I had my doubts. Old Luke also told me that in the days of his grandfather, Very Very Old Luke, Tripp Street was called "Pig Road" and boasted the finest pig farm in the county. A pig farm was an unlikely spot to find "God's Country." Especially for a rabbi.

But the moment a silver delivery truck with three black letters painted on the side pulled into my gravel driveway, I knew this was God's Country. The truck resolved an uncertainty gnawing at me for twenty years, ever since a Methodist minister, an Episcopal priest, and I had made a guest appearance on a national TV program to discuss Avery Corman's book *Oh, God!* We had assembled for a "lighthearted theological discussion" (producer's description). The producer, questioning his own faith in the subject matter, had a team of ten-year-old boys skilled in karate waiting in the wings. If our heavenly discussion plummeted earthwards, martial arts would be rushed on stage.

We were well into the discussion when the moderator turned to me and asked a question I could not answer: "Dan, what would happen if God appeared in your driveway?" Lights and cameras riveted on my face. Makeup dripped down my forehead, preparing to take a nosedive into my lap. I searched for a profoundly lighthearted witty remark. I waited for an inspiration. The producer waited. My mother's entire dinner party in Albany, New York, paused in the middle of their Baked Alaska and waited. Unfortunately a glitch in communications gave out the incorrect date in Albany. Instead of watching *Oh, God!* Albany viewed a program on transvestites. After that, Albany lost her interest. But the rest of the Northeast waited for the answer to the question "What would happen if God appeared in your driveway?" They waited—but I was silent. Where had the producer found that question? The longest moment I have ever endured ended when the announcer cut in: "Just as our guest would be speechless if he found God in his driveway, you will be speechless when you taste our crispier, more delectable Snappy Crackers—and they will remain fresh for an eternity." (At least one of us was holding up the theological end!)

When the program ended, I vowed to research the question "What would happen if . . . ?" My search took me to esoteric texts, scribbled notes from classes at the seminary, the counsel of noted scholars. Of course, none of these sources gave answers. God seemed quite at home up there above the clouds, and no one wished to speculate on what would happen if He made a guest appearance in my driveway.

Years passed. "What would happen if . . ." continued to elude my grasp until the day we closed on the house on Tripp Street. We left our lawyer's office in midafternoon clutching the deed that proved we really owned an 1861 farmhouse. My wife was ecstatic. "Dan, let's spend the night at home, on Tripp Street."

I protested. "We don't have furniture, the electricity's shut off, we'll freeze!" But Marion persisted. "Please, please." So we drove up Murphy's Hill, skidding on a patch of ice, and pulled into RD3 Tripp Street. Icicles hung precariously from the roof as we disappeared into the empty house. Only the cold floorboards creaked a greeting. I mused on memories fallen beneath the cracks of those pine boards. Had the pig farmer stood on this spot? George Carpenter, who shot down the electric wires chasing chicken thieves? One hundred thirty years of footsteps leaving their own imprint on the floor of my home. Then suddenly Marion called from the den, "Dan, you wouldn't believe it. God is in the driveway." I couldn't believe it. After all these years? An answer to my question? "What would happen if . . . ?" Impossible! Marion must be overly excited. The thrill of our new home. But— what if? Shouldn't I be open to miracles? Feeling slightly foolish, I walked out on the driveway and there they were. Black letters glistening off silver metal. Black letters. GOD. God was in my driveway, emblazoned on the side of a giant delivery truck. GOD. And if God could appear on the side of the truck, who knew what wonders lay within. My reflections were interrupted by a burly truck driver who descended from the cab and spoke in a dialect distinctly New York. He was not Gabriel, Michael, Raphael, or any of the other angels associated with God.

"Hey, buddy," his voice called out. "What kind of street you got here? When you going to fix the potholes?" As if I could fix the potholes!

"Can I help you?" I asked.

"Buddy, I'm here with your bed and quilt. Where d'yuh want 'em?"

"What?"

"The bed and quilt. From Bloomingdale's."

Who was this man delivering furniture in a truck marked GOD? Did he know of my unending quest for God in the driveway? Tentatively I approached the driver.

"Excuse me. This is a bit strange. Here you are in my driveway with a truck marked GOD but you are only delivering furniture. Could you explain? Who is GOD? Or what is GOD?"

The driver laughed. "Don't you know? GOD stands for Guaranteed Overnight Delivery—1-800-DIAL-GOD. Get it? GOD. Yep, we get things to you overnight. GOD."

And maybe he was God, at least for Marion and myself spending the first night on Tripp Street in an 1861 farmhouse without heat. Yes, maybe one bed and a down quilt did represent God, or a gift from God. I can't be sure, but after that experience I no longer search for God in esoteric texts or lofty places. Now I search closer to home and find what I am seeking in earthly realms. In a delivery truck marked GOD, a grandfather clock, the dusty pages of a book, a golden butterfly skimming the daisies. And in the seasons. The forsythia announcing spring and the promise of a newly born child; the warmth of summer and the blossoming of love; a solitary red maple leaf awakening memories of journeys past; footprints on a winter landscape as the spirit anticipates rebirth.

And if it's true of God, perhaps it's true of all those big words we pursue through life: fulfillment, happiness, contentment, meaning. They are as near as the eye can see or the hand can touch. If only we would open our eyes to wonders greeting us from little things, daily events, our families, the people we know. On my street, Tripp Street. On your street. In an 1861 farmhouse. In a glass contemporary house overlooking Murphy's Hill. Fulfillment, happiness, contentment, meaning, even God within our grasp. If we look. If we listen.

So now as I sit on the wall and Old Luke passes by, we exchange greetings and he chuckles. "Well, Dan, which is it? A pig farm or 'God's Country'?" I smile. "God's Country, Old Luke. God's Country. GOD."

2. Sheldon the Sniffing Beagle

God's Country does not guarantee faith.

Once I was a trusting soul. Now I have filed trust in a steamer trunk with Old English, *Beowulf,* Chaucer, and Shakespeare. It's hard to have perfect trust. We just don't live in a trusting world. Not even in God's Country. And my suspicions peaked when I met Sheldon the Sniffing Beagle.

In all fairness, Sheldon did not spawn suspicion. It began when I fell in love with the old farmhouse, tethered my Toyota to a brass ring in the stone wall (where an earlier generation tied up horses), and in a burst of exuberance shouted, "I'll take it!" My wife, a real estate agent, quickly pulled in my reins and asked appropriate questions. "Dan, how do we know the house is sound? First we need an engineer, then we have to test the water, muck out the septic tank, inspect the soil for contamination, hunt for asbestos, measure radon—"

I interrupted my wary wife. "Nonsense, Marion. I remember when my parents bought their house on South Main Avenue. They simply shook hands with the prior owners and lived happily ever after. Why are you so suspicious?"

Marion smiled. "Dan, you have too much faith." And I guess my wife was right. Somewhere in my genes, perhaps because I am a second-generation clergyman, I believe in the essential goodness nestled inside every man and woman. But these are the 1990s, and occasionally, just occasionally, the world is not as I would like it to be. Better to be cautious. Extra security never hurts.

Picking up the phone, I called Ray's Radon Inc.; Sweety's "We Rush So You Can Flush" Septic Associates; The ABC Asbestos Busting Company; Sanitary Dirt and Sons; and Well, Well Water.

Then our lawyer threw in a personal caveat: "Why is the prior owner selling?"

I replied, "She died."

The lawyer shuddered. "What was the cause of death?"

I didn't know.

"Go down to White Plains and obtain a death certificate. We have to know the cause of death."

Suspicions are contagious. Driving to White Plains, I envisioned the worst. Perhaps she died from remnants of bubonic plague carried over from the old country when the house was built in 1861; ghosts of Christmas Past; a killer bunny. Hyperventilating, I climbed to the fourth floor of the County Court House and forced out the words: "Please, the death certificate of Matilda McMiggins." The clerk rummaged through official records and handed me the document.

New York State Department of Health—Certificate of Death. Matilda McMiggins died May 17, 1984, at Memorial Hospital. Age of de-

ceased—99. To the best of my knowledge death occurred of natural causes resulting from old age. Signed: Dr. R. Blake

A normal death certificate. Unless you are a victim of the suspicion virus. Every word blinked a warning signal. Matilda McMiggins? Well, that probably was her name. But the phrase "To the best of my knowledge death occurred of natural causes resulting from old age." "To the best of my knowledge." Room for doubt. Why didn't the doctor write, "Matilda *definitely* died of old age," or "Beyond a reasonable doubt." Could there be some deep dark mystery in ninety-nine-year-old Matilda's death? "To the best of my knowledge." Not a sufficient guarantee.

I called my lawyer. "Hank, do you think there is a problem?" Hank assured me he would search out the details, and I returned home for the final test. Termites.

Tom Barnes's Ford pickup, with the words "Getting Out the Bugs Exterminators" emblazoned on fire-engine-red doors, pulled in behind me. Tom had been working in our neighborhood for over thirty years, and even the termites testified to his talent and determination. When Tom was around, termites were terminal. Tom Barnes browsed for about an hour, looking under the beams, tapping on ancient supporting posts fashioned out of tree trunks, shining his flashlight in between the floorboards.

"Not a termite around," Tom said. I detected a note of disappointment in his voice.

That night we met Bob and Marcia for dinner and reported on our progress. "Almost ready to sign the contract. Septic, radon, asbestos, termites, all tested out well."

"Termites?" Marcia asked. "Termites? Who inspected for termites?"

"Getting Out the Bugs."

Marcia shrugged. "They're okay, but I'll tell you, they missed the termites at the Larsons' house."

"Missed the termites?"

"Yep. Next time you drive by look at the deck. Leaning to portside. Termites. If you want to be certain, call Sheldon the Sniffing Beagle. He doesn't miss a termite."

I looked at Marcia quizzically. "Sheldon the Sniffing Beagle? You must be kidding."

But I knew. Marcia never kids. "I don't have the details, but some exterminator, I think he's located off the Interboro Parkway, has a beagle that can smell termites."

That night I couldn't sleep. I tried counting termites leaping over fences, but the termites didn't leap. They ate through. Early the next morning I called Marcia.

"How do I get in touch with Sheldon?" Marcia located the number and at 9:00 A.M. I was on the phone with Woody, Sheldon's owner.

"Hello, Woody. This is Dan. I want to talk to you about Sheldon."

If termites are into wood, Woody was into Sheldon.

"Best darn sniffer in the world," he began. "Used to work for the cops in the South Bronx. The narcs. Sheldon sniffed out marijuana, crack, heroin. Then at the age of seven Sheldon went through a mid-life crisis. Couldn't take the heat of working the South Bronx. He wasn't eating. Wasn't barking. Lost his interest in Grace the blond Yorkie up the street. So I sent him to school in California to become a termite sniffer. Now he's happy again. He loves working in the suburbs. Doesn't miss the city. Not a bit."

I contracted for Woody and Sheldon to come to town immediately but encountered a series of delays. First, Sheldon was in California. "I had to send him back for his six-month checkup. If he's around humans too long, he loses his sense of smell. Humans do that to you. But Sheldon will be back on Monday. Tuesday okay?"

Tuesday was fine, but on Tuesday morning Woody called. "I've got the stomach flu. Better change the appointment to Wednesday."

Wednesday, Woody called again. He was feeling fine but Sheldon had a cold. "Stuffed nose. Can't smell a thing."

Finally, on Thursday, Woody and Sheldon the Sniffing Beagle made their appearance at my farmhouse. A cute little guy. White with brown spots (Sheldon, not Woody) and floppy ears. Still a bit jet-lagged from the trip to California, Sheldon plodded through the kitchen, the living room, the dining room. Suddenly his ears stood on end and his nose plunged to the floor. Woody beamed.

"Good boy, Sheldon. Good boy."

I looked at Marion. She looked at me. Woody looked at both of us. Then, in a tone honed by years of experience, he pronounced the gloomy verdict: "Termites down there."

"Impossible," I said. "Getting Out the Bugs gave us a clean bill of health."

"Then why did you call me?" Woody asked. "Suspicious?"

He sure had my number.

"How do you know there are termites?"

Woody fixed me with a piercing look. "See that nose go down? Sheldon smells the methane the termites are giving off. Believe me. After a stay in California his reconditioned sniffer wouldn't miss methane. Not a chance. And look at Sheldon's ears. Straight up. He hears the termite mandibles."

I looked puzzled. "Don't you know about mandibles?" Woody went on. "That's termite terminology. Let me recommend a book you can read on termites. Good summer reading. Has pictures too. In the meantime take my word for it; termites have these things called mandibles. They're like jaws. Soldier termites stand guard and click their mandibles when danger approaches. And Sheldon's danger!"

By this time I didn't know who to believe. Getting Out the Bugs? Woody? Sheldon the Sniffing Beagle? Only one way to find out if I had termites. Rip up the floor. Woody grabbed a crowbar from his black bag and pried loose a section. There they were! An army of termites turned sluggish from a day of

OD'ing on pine board junk food. Sheldon snarled. Woody beamed. I fainted.

That night Marion and I huddled. Should we buy the house? Woody had promised the foundation could be treated, but the underpinnings of my psychological foundation had crumbled into dust. Sawdust! Finally we bought the house, with one proviso: I have signed Sheldon the Sniffing Beagle to a lifetime contract. Every three months he travels to my house for a routine checkup, but I must admit I am suspicious. Is Sheldon really doing his job or am I being used by a beagle in search of a country home? Should I move into the condos springing up on Wastelands Valley Road? Why is the road called Wastelands Valley? Are the condos built on a toxic dump site? How can I find out? Anyway, are termites also moving into condos? And my lawyer still hasn't returned my call on Matilda McMiggins. Did she or did she not die of old age? Did my lawyer die of old age? Will Sheldon die of old age? Do termites ever die? Oh, dear! Oh, dear! When I use my can of hair spray am I enlarging the hole in the ozone layer? Is global warming worse than nuclear winter? What if my born-again faith in suspicion does not guarantee peace of mind? What if—

And Marion, poor Marion, has to tolerate my suspicions. Despite her reassurances. "Dan, we investigated thoroughly. Did every test. That's enough. There aren't any absolutes in life. Nothing is certain. Nothing. You can't always question."

I'm trying. Trying to return to my roots as a second-generation man of faith. Trying to face each day in spite of the termites of doubt gnawing at my heart. Because Marion's right. She's always right. We have to live our lives. With or without certainties. With or without termites.

3. This Rabbi's a Truck-Drivin' Man

———— ~⌒~ ————

When did I first know that I wanted to drive a truck?

The year was 1959, the same year I entered the seminary to prepare for a lifetime career as a rabbi. I was chugging along U.S. 1 on my Vespa when an eighteen-wheeler hit me with a blast of exhaust fumes that forced me off the highway. From that day on I longed to drive above the world in the cab of an interstate van. I never went public with this fantasy. My friends would laugh at me. How many clergymen want to barrel down U.S. 1? Then I turned fifty and realized I was traveling around a major bend in the road, my life clearly shifting into mid-life crisis. It was now or never.

But where do you find a truck? I contemplated renting one, but my rational nature intervened: "You rent a truck only when you have something to put into the truck." I do carry volumes of books, a yellow pad, and extra pencils or pens from my home to my study, but did I need a twelve-, fifteen-, or eighteen-foot truck van for the accouterments of the mind?

When I moved into the house on Tripp Street opportunity beckoned. A giant Atlas moving van (even the name sent shivers through my body) pulled up. I approached the truck with a certain feeling of intimacy. This was not just any truck. After all, that was my bed resting comfortably in the hold. Perhaps I could ask the driver if I might borrow the truck and take my bed for a spin. I rushed back to the house in pursuit of the truckers. They were trying to straighten a mattress pretzeled around the second-floor landing. I knew from the steady stream of expletives floating down the stairway that these truckers would not be responsive to my deep-seated needs. Slowly the van emptied. My spirits sagged. Soon the van would disappear, taking with it my load of dreams. But, as occasionally happens in life, chance intervened. My wife was speaking with the driver.

"My husband and I still have some furniture stored upstate. Never had room for it in the old house. Four or five pieces." She described them in detail. "Do you ever work in the Albany area?"

"Ma'am," the driver said, "we go anywhere, but let me make a suggestion. You don't even have a thousand pounds in Albany. Save yourself four or five hundred dollars; have your husband rent a truck and drive up to the warehouse."

Lurking behind a maple tree, I overheard destiny call.

Early next morning I called Ryder Truck Rental. "How large a truck do I need for a Sheraton dresser, a highboy, a corner cabinet, and several cane chairs?"

The man at the other end of the line thought for a minute. "Sounds like two loads in a station wagon. Got a station wagon?"

"No," I lied. I'd be damned if some anonymous dispatcher at Ryder would squelch my plans!

"Well then, maybe a pickup would do. But *we* don't have any. Try Bobby's Rent All."

Bobby's Rent All? That's where I rented my Snappy Boy lawn mower. Real men don't rent trucks from Bobby's Rent All. But I was desperate. I called Bobby's. Joe answered.

"Joe, I've got to bring a big load down from Albany; moving job I'm on. Might be able to fit it into a twelve-footer, but probably a fifteen-footer would be better. Got any around?"

"Sure. Come on over at nine tomorrow morning."

That night I couldn't sleep. At 5:00 A.M. I began to assemble the proper truckin' clothes.

"Marion," I called to my wife, "have you seen my Levi's?"

Marion groaned from underneath the white cotton percale sheets covering our bed.

"Your Levi's? I haven't seen them since we were married."

That was many years ago. So I settled for a pair of corduroys with a worn crotch, a down vest, patches advertising Zermatt and Vail, Gore-Tex hiking boots, and departed for Bobby's.

Bobby's Rent All threw me into the computer, duly recorded my American Express Card number, and escorted me to the truck.

"Top of the line. A Ford, only has forty-three hundred miles on it, not a spot of grease."

They were right. Clean as a whistle. I could have worn my gray three-piece suit.

Joe asked, "You want to take out insurance? Covers everything but the roof."

"The roof? What could happen to the roof? You mean if pigeons soil the paint or something?"

"I mean if you go under a bridge that's lower than ten feet, ten inches." And so I became a trucker.

Backing out of the parking lot offered my first challenge. A box blocked my rearview mirror. A giant fifteen-foot box. American trucks. Not worth a cent. I was sure the Japanese

would have invented a see-through truck, or at least a computerized voice: "Key is in the ignition. An obstruction is in the
rearview mirror. Do not proceed backwards past Park Place."

Joe watched my plight from the window of Bobby's Rent
All and (after a good laugh) escorted me out of the lot. Time
for a coffee break and strategy. How could I drive from Westchester County to Albany, New York, and return without shifting into reverse? How did eighteen-wheelers back into
driveways? Perhaps in time I would join the elite who traversed
life backwards and blindly, but not today. Not yet.

As I inched my way up Route 22 and onto 684, I experi-
enced the sort of divine revelation that delights clergy. I had
made it! Above the world. Or at least above the lowly BMW
racing me to a yield sign. But who was I to yield? Not me. Not
a trucker. Anyway, I was insured, except for the roof, and not
a BMW in the world could reach my roof. Near Newburgh I
edged up to the bumper of a Dodge Colt and let out a mighty
blast on my horn. The Colt shimmied and bolted to one side.
I doffed my imaginary Phillips 66 hat and resolved to buy the
proper head covering at the next truck stop.

On the New York Thruway I tuned in to country music,
"I'll Play on My Banjo If You'll Give Me Your Heart," and
remembered the times interstate trucks rushed past and flicked
their cigarettes onto my roof. I didn't smoke, but I aimed a
piece of thoroughly chewed sugarless gum. Bull's-eye! The gum
splattered on the windshield of a red Subaru!

By the time I reached Albany, the Ford had digested a
tankful of gasoline. I pulled into a Mobil station, began to
execute a tight right turn (routine for my Toyota), but forgot
the extra fifteen feet on Bobby's Rent All. A nervous Mobil
serviceman remembered. Displaying courage under fire, he
pushed against my headlights. This act of laying on of hands
seized my attention, sparing two bright blue and white Mobil
gas pumps decapitation. I slid off the seat, my knees shaking.

"Don't worry," I said. "I'm insured for everything but the roof."

"Don't know what you're talking about," he said, "but I'd guess you haven't been driving one of those rigs very long."

I reared up in anger. "Nonsense. It's been more than an hour."

The Mobil man kept his distance as I pulled out of his lot with a question: "Those overhead electrical wires are more than ten feet ten, aren't they?"

Down the road from Mobil I drove into the parking lot of Albany Moving and Storage Company. The dispatcher signaled me to park between two vans, eighteen-wheelers that dwarfed Bobby's Rent All. Humbly I slid out of my seat, hoping the loyal Ford would not be cowed by its larger relatives.

The warehouse men unsealed my crate of furniture and asked if I needed help.

"Don't worry," I said, "it's under a thousand pounds, but if you're free, you might just lift it onto the end of the truck. I can do the rest." The men tossed the furniture onto the truck. Two hours later I had pushed, pulled, and coaxed the pieces into the far corner of the van, where I looped eighty-two yards of hemp around the antique pieces. The maze of rope would have earned the admiration of a spider. Only the highboy, perched in the rear of the load, faced 150 miles of imminent danger.

The trip home progressed without incident, except for periodic stops when I would disappear into the bowels of the truck, inspect the rope, and reassure the highboy, "Don't worry. We're almost home—and yes, we are having a good time."

An hour out of Westchester I called my wife. "Should be off the road in time for dinner. You might hire a couple of boys from the high school to help unload."

Under a veil of darkness I arrived home. John and his friend Pee Wee (a diminutive high school student shorter than the highboy but with more pickup than the Ford from Bobby's Rent

All) helped unload. Within ten minutes they had placed each piece of furniture in place.

"You fellows are lucky," I said. "Getting this stuff off the truck is a breeze. You should've been with me in Albany!"

My wife called from the den. "Pull the truck into the driveway and we'll relax. Channel Thirteen has a special. The American Ballet Theatre."

I declined. "I think I'll return the truck tonight. Let 'em know I completed the trip and the roof's all right."

"That's ridiculous," my wife said. "You've done enough work for one day."

How could I admit that if I pulled the truck into the driveway for the night I'd never be able to back out in the morning! Who wanted a fifteen-foot truck on the front lawn of our farmhouse for the next thirty years? So I returned the van to Bobby's Rent All. But I had fulfilled my dream. Soared above the heavens, rolling over Vespas on U.S. 1. Truck driver for a day!

Eventually all of us climb down from the van of dreams. Our feet touch the ground of reality where we live out life. But I will never be the same. Look at me! Covered with a golden aura. I did it! Only once. But I did it. New York to Albany. Above the world. And I never drove in reverse! Just call me Dan, the truck-drivin' man.

4. When the Books and I Came Home

Even when we move we take the past. For me that past was stored in seventy-five cartons of books. Frank, the burly driver for Regan's Moving, had unloaded the furniture, then started on the books—more than two thousand volumes packed in boxes from the local liquor store.

I wondered about packing books in liquor cartons. Do liquor and reading mix? I placed a complete set of Robert Burns's poetry in an empty Johnnie Walker carton and stepped back. Not a bad match! A Scottish poet in a carton of Scotch. Packing became a challenge; pair books and boxes. Dostoyevski felt right at home traveling inside Smirnoff Vodka. Mark Twain? His down-home tales appreciated bouncing from side to side in a carton of Jack Daniel's Tennessee Sour Mash Whiskey. And the history of the Napoleonic wars lapped up their journey in a case of Beaujolais.

Frank did not appreciate my grand design. Instead, after carrying the seventy-fifth carton, he shook his head in disbelief. "Don't know anyone who could read all these." But then Frank, of Regan's Moving, didn't know Dad. This was his library, and I'll wager that he had read every one of the books. The books with pictures. The books without pictures. Ancient texts with brown tattered covers. A parchment scroll. My father, a rabbi, was seldom seen without a book, and when I was only three he had already started my library with an illustrated *Winnie-the-Pooh* and *Robinson Crusoe*. From there we moved on to *Andersen's Fairy Tales* and *The Arabian Nights*. Dad would sit in the yellow wing chair with Hoppy, our Boston terrier, nestled by his feet and read me the story of Sinbad the Sailor. In the company of Persian kings in red robes and yellow turbans, Sinbad, my father, and I sailed to the Indies. According to legend, Sinbad had inherited his father's fortune and amused himself by travel. My inheritance was a journey with Gulliver, King Arthur, the Knights of the Round Table; and by the age of seven my collection of books spilled off the windowsill in my bedroom.

About the time I was tall enough to peek into the unabridged version of Webster's dictionary, majestic on a metal stand next to the fireplace, Dad approached me with a proposition: "Daniel, how would you like your own bookshelf in the living room?" And the next thing I knew Winnie, Robinson, Hans Christian, Gulliver, and Arthur squeezed onto a maple shelf between *Encyclopaedia Britannica* and *Famous Poets of the English Language*. Rather heavy company for my literary friends, but they fit in perfectly.

Whatever my particular interest, Dad always came up with the right book. For instance, during my high school days as a shortstop on the junior varsity, *The Babe Ruth Story* slid onto the shelf. Dad loved baseball and knew the batting averages of every New York Yankee, Baltimore Oriole, and Albany Senator (our hometown team). According to Aunt Ida, "Your father was a great pitcher when he was young. Could have played for the Yankees." Instead he traded the pinstripes of the diamond for the pinstripes of the clergy. But he sure knew a good baseball book! Off the field, my father's library got me through English class (*The House of the Seven Gables*), American History (*John Adams and the American Revolution*), and even German (*Jacobowsky and the Colonel*).

Graduation. Alan's parents gave him cuff links with the initials A.S.; Wayne got a shirt and tie. Naturally, my present, wrapped in blue paper with a fluffy bow, was a book. And so I welcomed John Bartlett and his *Familiar Quotations* to my library. Inside the cover Dad had written an inscription: "To Daniel—With the hope that you and your books will be lasting partners! Love, Dad."

I still use Bartlett's, exploring the 18,000 quotes from Aesop to Yeats, the sparks of my father's love of books.

And with this upbringing, you can understand why books have been so important in my life, why I beamed as Regan's Moving unloaded the seventy-fifth carton of books. The two thousand volumes have kept my father alive. And that is what he wanted some thirty years ago when he called me into his study several weeks before the last chapter of his life would draw to a close. We talked. "Daniel, do you know what you want to do with your life?"

I didn't hesitate. "I want to become a rabbi. Like you."

My father smiled with satisfaction. "Someday you may change your mind, but whatever you decide, I have one request. My books. Take care of them for another generation." Dad's eyes scanned the room where he had spent a lifetime reading or writing sermons on three-by-five pieces of yellow paper. The orange Parker pen leaked onto the blotter. Outside a gaggle of geese departed on their winter pilgrimage.

Following our conversation, my father's strength ran out, and I stood by his grave near a meadow on the outskirts of Albany where young colts gamboled in the morning sun. Years passed. My mother moved to a small apartment and I received my inheritance. Dad's books. Since I lived in a renovated one-room red schoolhouse complete with locusts but no bookshelves, Dad's library was sent to storage. Then, at age thirty-six, I married and moved into my wife's home, a Cape Cod with blue and white shutters. Marion already had two children—two dogs (a French poodle and an illiterate Irish setter)—and very little room for books. Eventually I redeemed the books and stacked them in the basement on rough pine shelves. Three deep. Inaccessible.

The first month after we settled into the Cape I made a trip to the basement to visit the books. Let them know someone cared! I can't pass a book without settling in and thumbing through the pages. (Probably a genetic family trait!) Choosing a book on archeology, *Rivers in the Desert*, written by a friend of my father's when they were students at the seminary, I stretched out on the cement floor. Near the end of the first chapter, faded index cards hidden in the binding fluttered to the floor like golden leaves on an autumn landscape. I had discovered Dad's notes spinning the magic of a voyage he and the archeologist took in the Holy Land along the river valleys of the Sinai Desert. Wandering on paths of memory, I did not feel the water trickling under my feet. At first only a tiny rivulet, then a steady flow. Heavy rains had swelled an underground spring and forced water up cellar cracks. My basement was approaching flood stage and Dad's books, the precious tie to a past, had become an endangered species. This arrangement would never work.

Only a family of field mice seemed happy with the sprawling mound of books. They stored a winter's supply of nuts between the stacks. In fairness to the mice, they liked books. One especially precocious little fellow nibbled at Whitman's

Leaves of Grass, a fine choice for a mouse. Every spring I cleaned out the mice, packing them off with their nutshells, and dreamed of a day when I could live surrounded by books in every room, a house with space for my father's library.

. . .

Tripp Street. The moving men finished unloading. I thanked Frank and gave him an appropriate tip: a copy of *The Travels of Marco Polo.* Frank gave me a strange look and began his travels back downtown.

I plunged into unpacking the cartons. Sandburg's *Abraham Lincoln* found a place in the hall of the Civil War farmhouse; travel books and Adirondack lore line shelves in the den; Americana and poetry are in the living room nestled beneath wooden beams. Whenever I gently blow the dust off one of my father's books or open the covers, he is with me, reading, "In the days of Sinbad the Sailor"; clearing space on his bookshelf; sharing his last moments in the study where his pen ran dry. He is with me, memories running as a deep stream.

We have come home.

5. Mrs. Martha Parsons

Permit me to introduce my lovely neighbor, Mrs. Martha Parsons. Rather, permit Mrs. Martha Parsons to introduce herself.

It was a winter day when Mrs. Martha Parsons in high heels and black gloves sloshed over our soggy front lawn followed by Sylvester, a gray (once black) toy poodle. Mrs. Martha Parsons, ninety-five years of age, and Sylvester, fourteen dog years, ninety-eight human years, had come to pay a courtesy call.

"I hope I am not interrupting, but I wish to welcome you to Tripp Street." Mrs. Parsons had been welcoming residents of Tripp Street since 1915, when she and Mr. Malcolm Parsons moved into the area. "We came the day Sophie's house burned down. Did you know Sophie? I suppose not. She died in 1922.

What a shame. Sophie and I played tennis together. She had a marvelous serve."

Mrs. Martha Parsons apologized for bringing Sylvester. "But you don't have to be afraid. She doesn't bite. I couldn't leave her home. We just came from the doctor."

"The doctor? I hope you're all right."

"I'm just fine. We were at Sylvester's doctor. I am afraid Sylvester is showing her age. Refuses to eat. Dr. Bernard gave her some pep pills. They cost a hundred dollars. Mr. Wolk, do you think it is worth a hundred dollars to stay young? That is, if they work. Oh, I do hope the pills work. Growing old is not for sissies."

While Mrs. Parsons spoke, Sylvester disappeared into the kitchen, returning with a fudge brownie from the counter. Mrs. Parsons blushed. "Oh, I'm so embarrassed. I don't know how Sylvester reached those brownies." Then reality struck. Sylvester had jumped onto a three-foot-high stool and from the stool onto the counter. Mrs. Martha Parsons clapped her hands together. "The pep pills work. Dr. Bernard! The man's a saint!" Suddenly Mrs. Parsons glanced at her watch and, leaning on her cane, started for the front door. "We don't want to overstay our welcome, and I must take Sylvester home. She always naps after she eats. But please come to visit. Come soon."

We came. Marion and I. Mrs. Martha Parsons was thrilled. We also brought our dog, Teddy, to play with Sylvester. Sylvester wasn't thrilled. At ninety-eight, dogs don't play. Even dogs popping pep pills. Mrs. Parsons lived in a gray colonial house framed by a boxwood hedge. Ushering us into a living room where heavy drapes shaded the sun, Mrs. Parsons asked, "Would you like tea or a cocktail?" It was one of those days where I had officiated at two baby namings, one wedding, and a funeral. I needed a Scotch. Chivas Regal. Johnnie Walker Red. But when I saw the watercress sandwiches (half consumed by Sylvester), propriety won out. "Tea, please. With lemon."

Mrs. Parsons smiled. "Tea is perfect for a winter day. Dorothy, a cup of tea for the gentleman." Then, turning back to me, Mrs. Martha Parsons said, "I hope you don't mind if I have a dry martini. I've been at the church since 7:00 A.M. setting up for the potluck dinner."

We sat in a living room exquisitely decorated with rococo and neoclassical furniture, intricately carved in flower and leaf designs. I sipped my tea. My hostess sipped her martini, and together we looked at photographs she had taken on many Grand Tours. There she sat astride a camel, the Pyramids in the background; there dressed in a pith helmet and bouncing on an elephant in India; there on an Amazon riverboat. "That was a fascinating trip. I was eighty-seven and caught two piranha!"

I laughed. "Have you run out of places to visit?"

A distant look appeared in Mrs. Parsons's eyes. "Not too long ago I was worried. Where else could I go? Then they started changing the names of all those countries. I read all about it in *Foreign Affairs* magazine. Upper Volta became Burkina Faso; Burma, Myanmar; Ceylon, Sri Lanka. Now I can start all over!"

Her mood changed. "I can't really travel anymore. The last trip I went on was in January with Sybil. She's my oldest great-grandchild. Did you know I have twenty-three great-grandchildren? Sybil took me on her sled in the backyard, but I couldn't stay out long. Too cold. Strange, when I was young I traveled everywhere in an open carriage. Didn't get cold then. My daughter says I'm aging, but I don't feel it. There are no lines on my spirit. I'm ninety-five years young, and sometimes that's more hopeful than forty years old."

Dusk embraced the house, and Sylvester, satiated from watercress sandwiches, snored softly on a pillow. As Marion and I rose to leave, Sylvester raised her head from the pillow, and I read the green lettering embroidered by Mrs. Parsons's daughter in honor of her mother's ninety-fifth birthday. "We Grow

Old By Not Growing." Mrs. Martha Parsons did not need the pillow. At least not the advice. And as long as the blessing of life was granted to her, Mrs. Parsons would keep growing.

Good evening, Mrs. Martha Parsons. Good evening. Until morning.

6. Teddy of
Hopeless Junction

~~~⊙~~~

Why did I ever permit Teddy to move into the house on Tripp Street?

I come from a long line of dog purists. Or pure doggists. As a child, the dogs we owned reeked of canine credentials. First there was our Old English sheepdog, offspring of Fezziwig Ceiling Zero. Then a Boston terrier, St. James of Abigail Bournemouth. And the springer spaniel, Lucksworth Sebastian Sunnymeade the Third. So, raised on the Who's Who of Woof Woof, how did I end up with Teddy of Hopeless Junction drooling by the side of my antique Hitchcock rocker? Teddy of Hopeless Junction. A mutt.

A more serious question. At the age of fifty-four, why do my wife and I again walk the path of life with a dog at the far end of the leash? Any dog. Our children have left the house, we are free to travel, and in bounds Teddy, hungry for Gaines-burger and a few pats. "Yes, Teddy, we'll be back soon. Please stay off the bed and don't howl. The neighbors are complaining!" Ah, yes, when I teach Holy Scriptures I read the divine word of caution. "To every thing there is a season, and a time to every purpose under the heaven" (Ecclesiastes, Chapter 3). A time for silence and a time for barking. But is this the time for a puppy? A mutt? Sure, a Yorkie or Lhasa, spiffy with a golden bow plaited in her hair, might be appropriate. But Teddy of Hopeless Junction? Slurping water from the swamp in back of our house and wearing a splattered red bandana? A muddy mutt?

How did it come about? In the beginning there was a phone call from a friend. An anguished voice at the other end pleaded, "If you believe action is more important than prayer, heed my words." The voice was quoting the line I used the week before in an awe-inspiring sermon.

"Jenny, that's terrific. A great imitation! Leaving the real estate business and going into preaching?"

"No, Dan. I'm serious. I have a dog in need. Homeless. Abandoned. Left to wander the four corners of the world on her four paws. Alone."

Jenny really laid it on.

"I know you and Marion vowed never to have another dog after Jenny." (Jenny, our late springer spaniel, not Jenny the real estate agent.) "But this puppy has already lived in three homes in seven months. A farmer in Pine Plains, then a family in Monroe, until the husband went off to prison, then . . ."

Jenny divulged the poor dog's sordid background before unleashing her final argument. "Having a puppy will keep you young!"

That was it. I could alleviate the homeless problem and avoid mid-life crisis with a single Yes.

THE DIRT FROM TRIPP STREET

I hesitated. "Jen, what breed of dog? You know when I was growing up, Fezziwig, St. James, and Lucksworth were household names."

Jen obviously didn't know, but with sensitivity described Teddy: "Her front half is Newfoundland, the back half black Lab. A real beauty." I envisioned an inverted black pyramid, broad at the head, tapering to a point near the rear.

"Visit Teddy," Jen implored. "No obligation. Just look." Jen knew my wife could not just look. And so, resigned to a new resident at our house on Tripp Street, I drove Marion to Pine Plains and exited from the car in time to be knocked into a snow pile by a fifty-pound bounding puppy. My first impression of Teddy remains the underside of her stomach as she licked my face and extended a paw. (To help me up?) Further inspection revealed a well-dressed Newfound-Lab wearing a basic black fur coat with a touch of white at the neckline.

"Jen, we'll give it a try. Her papers, please."

Jen looked puzzled, then she disappeared into the house and returned with a bundle of back issues of the *Pine Plains Post.* "You really won't need these newspapers. Teddy's almost housebroken."

Of course I meant Teddy's pedigree papers, papers she lost on a black night when a black Labrador met a black Newfoundland. I wondered, had I already forgotten Teddy's illicit background? For that matter, would I ever adjust to owning a mutt? Would I sound convincing when I explained to friends we had two dogs, a Newfoundland and a Lab, but they ran around together?

The first night, Teddy slept peacefully at the foot of our bed. I sat up most of the night blowing my nose and rubbing my eyes. Was I allergic? To Teddy? Nonsense! For fifty years dogs and I lived together. But in the morning I visited the allergist, a pediatrician who lived up the block. (She gave me a lollipop. Jen was correct. Teddy would keep me young.)

"Well? Am I allergic?"

"Off the scale," the doctor replied. "Highly allergic."

Triumphantly I returned home. I would tell Marion, "I tried, dear. Honestly. But we can't keep Teddy. You see, I'm allergic."

Marion sat in the kitchen brushing fleas off the puppy. The grocery closet, usually empty, was filled with cans of puppy chow. Blue balls with bells, white rubber balls, and assorted pet toys filled the countertop; and bowls of water turned the kitchen into a wetland. How could I break the news to Marion?

I didn't have to. Marion anticipated the doctor's report. "Dan, if you are allergic, why don't you sleep on the porch? I know it's cold, but you can have the quilt."

I couldn't be sure, but I intuited that Marion and Teddy were bonding well. Feeling rejected, I sought professional help from the town psychologist and for fifty minutes recalled early memories of Fezziwig, St. James, and Lucksworth Sebastian.

The doctor smiled, grunted, then pounced on my words. "Don't you realize? Teddy of Hopeless Junction collides with parental expectations engraved on the hidden recesses of your unconscious. Only the best. Only the pedigreed. You judge by the name and not by the dog! Fezziwig, Lucksworth, bah! You are a victim of canine snobbery manifest in sneezing and watering eyes. A casebook case, my friend. A casebook case."

"Well, Doctor, what do I do?"

The doctor thumbed through a dog-eared medical text.

"Dan, as you are aware, the mind influences the body. Many allergies trace their origins to emotional roots. Unable to accept a mutt in your life, you think you can sneeze her away. If you truly want to adjust to Teddy, think positively. Reflect on the love she brings into your home. Companionship. Acceptance. Loyalty. Focus on Teddy's positive qualities instead of her questionable background."

Then, handing me a bill and a box of Kleenex, he scheduled a second appointment, and I returned home to set up quarters on the porch.

Months have passed. The doctor and I worked diligently to overcome my allergy. After three sessions without a sneeze I was pronounced cured.

Just in time. I never would have made it through the winter. Once again Marion and I share a common quilt and listen to the gentle sounds of Teddy gnawing on the leg of the dining-room table or bathing in her water bowl.

Better yet, Teddy has found her way into my heart, putting Fezziwig Ceiling, Lucksworth Sebastian, and St. James of Abigail to shame. Granted, Teddy will never appear in the Social Register or even wear a diamond-studded blanket for the cold days of winter. But those are only externals. Underneath the leaves and mud (from rolling in the swamp) covering Teddy's matted fur lies a loving, nuzzling, affectionate friend, Teddy of Hopeless Junction. What's in a name? Nothing. Neither pedigree, progenitor, nor parentage determines the quality of a dog. And more: My acceptance of Everydog now extends to Everyman. And Everywoman. Gone are the days when I judge anyone by their name or background or social status. If you wish to discover the real worth, look beneath the fur, or the skin.

And when Teddy and I walk on Tripp Street, sniffing our way from tree to tree, and passersby comment, "How cute. Is she a Lab or a—?" I interrupt and my chest swells with pride as I answer, "Meet Teddy. A mutt. A mongrel. A mixed breed." And Teddy of Hopeless Junction barks in agreement.

7. The Bird Feeder

When peace comes, it will be ushered in on my bird feeder. Certain political pundits pondering peace suggest that recent events in Eastern Europe presage an era of peace; soon the Messiah will ride through the Brandenburg Gate on a white donkey. I know differently. The age of peace will not arrive until the occupants of my bird feeder get their act together.

I reached this conclusion immediately after settling in at the farmhouse. While my wife pondered the proper location for the Sheraton dresser and Hitchcock rocker, I stalked the grounds for a proper bird-feeding site. Outside the kitchen window, hemlock branches waved in the morning breeze. On the top branches robins arranged twigs for a nest; purple grackles occupied the middle range of branches. Obviously the tree was a favorite haunt for birds. By midday one bird feeder and two suet cakes dangled from the hemlock, and I waited for the birds of Tripp Street to dine at their fly-in restaurant.

A word about my bird feeder. It has been with me for over a half dozen years. For all those years the feeder, a cylindrical container crowned by a plastic hood, successfully fended off squirrels. After years of catering to the dietary needs of birds, I know the danger of squirrels invading a bird feeder. Once a squirrel cracks the sunflower seed code and devises a method for access to the feeder, birds face a winter of despair or soup kitchens. Fortunately my feeder is squirrel-proof. Or was. In the good old days a squirrel jumped onto the plastic hood, slid off, and after rearranging his (or her) ruffled tail went next door, where Wayne feeds all God's children.

That is why, after filling the feeder, I sat back with confidence and waited for the birds. In the meantime the local squirrel population, unaware that I possessed a squirrel-proof bird feeder, huddled below and planned strategy. I studied my adversaries. There was old Scarface. According to the neighbors, Scarface received his wound from Fat Charley, who, tradition held, could finish off a five-pound bag of sunflower seeds in a single day. I was skeptical. No squirrel can consume five pounds a day. Further research revealed that Fat Charley had a seed concession at the Bronx Zoo. Then there was Skinny. Skinny wasn't always skinny, but ever since he ate my neighbor's plastic bird feeder in a frenzied quest for the elusive thistle, Skinny has been troubled with gastroenterological problems. Poor squirrel. A lesson to all those too deeply into plastics! Calling the signals was Roberto the Red, a red squirrel one quarter the size of Fat Charley. But mean. Real mean. None of the gray squirrels fooled around with Roberto the Red.

As chickadees flew tentatively onto the perches and began to peck away at the sunflower seed, the squirrel huddle broke. Fat Charley scrambled up the hemlock. Gleefully I waited for him to pounce on the plastic hood covering the feeder and plummet earthwards. But Fat Charley didn't tip the scales at five pounds six ounces because of thyroid or metabolism problems. No, sir! Fat Charley was fat because he ravaged every bird feeder in the neighborhood, squirrel-proof or not! And Fat Charley knew if you can't beat them over the table, deal under the table. Before I could say "bird seed," Fat Charley had leaped from the tree, flew *under* the hood, and dangled on a bird perch. He teetered for a moment, then gained control. But instead of eating, Fat Charley leaped back onto the trunk of the hemlock and repeated his performance. This was too much! After five or six times Charley could jump backwards, frontwards, holding on with one paw, eyes closed. Having perfected the technique, Charley settled in to a sunflower seed meal. On the limbs above, the chickadees raised a chorus of protest, but what could I do? While Fat Charley shook seed onto the ground for Scarface and Skinny, I rolled out the anti-squirrel artillery.

Anyone plagued by squirrels on the bird feeder knows the standard defensive tactics. First I greased the feeder. Then I tacked "Posted" signs on the hemlock and installed an audio-cassette. Instructions for squirrel stew blared across the countryside: "First catch a squirrel . . ." Nothing worked. Fat Charley sat on the feeder facing the kitchen window, extended his tongue in my direction, and spit shells. (My wife cautioned me not to take Charley's antics personally, but I have recently raised the bounty for Charley's head from twenty-five to a hundred dollars.) Worse, Charley taught Skinny and Scarface his undercover tricks. The entire pack of squirrels leaped under the hood, quarreling over the choicest seeds.

Eventually the squirrels left and the birds enjoyed their moment in the sunflower. But even birds can't seem to feed together. A screeching blue jay terrorized the chickadees; a crow, on a flight pattern out of the northwest, crash-landed on a woodpecker buried in a peanut-butter-laced suet cake; a nuthatch descending the tree upside down collided with a tufted titmouse climbing right side up. I mused. How could I inform the birds, "Friends, there's enough food for everyone. Haven't

I overinvested in seed futures at Tony's Nursery? Have we not all one Feather? Has not one God created us?" But I knew, even if the birds and the squirrels grasped this kernel of truth, peace would not emerge. Among chickadees and blue jays, Fat Charley and Roberto the Red, someone would always want more. Political scientists call this phenomenon the seed-greed factor. And if the simplest of creatures, birds and squirrels, can't monitor their behavior, who can expect humans to act differently?

Three thousand years ago the biblical prophet Isaiah, dressed in white robes and sandals and carrying a staff, stumped through the countryside and preached to the children of Israel. "Oh man, the day will come when the lion and lamb will lie down together. Then peace will cover the face of the earth, as the waters cover the stream." That was three thousand years ago. Today no one expects a lion and a lamb to lie down together; certainly not in Westchester County, where lions are rare and lambs are usually reduced to chops. But whenever I look out my kitchen window and observe bird feeder wars, I am filled with the prophetic spirit. One of these days I will leap onto the countertop next to the microwave and summon my family or anyone else who ever questioned my sanity. Dressed in a Brooks Brothers white button-down robe, Ferragamo sandals, and carrying a Hammacher Schlemmer walking staff, I will exhort the multitude with my modest proposal for peace: "And it shall come to pass that the day will come when the squirrel and sparrow will sit together on a single perch. Then peace will cover the face of the earth like sunflower shells cover the ground."

And all the squirrels and all the birds will say, "Amen. Amen."

8. Human Contact Day

Human Contact Day falls on the night after the winter solstice.

Human Contact Day. Tripp Street's contribution to the betterment of humanity. A contribution reaching far beyond the four-tenths-mile length of Tripp Street.

Human Contact Day. Occurring on the shortest day of the year. When Christians and Jews celebrate Christmas and Hanukkah, bringing light to darkness. Of all the unique days on the Tripp Street calendar, Human Contact Day is the most recent. My brainchild. Inaugurated after a phone conversation with my neighbor Hank.

On the eighth day of Hanukkah, a week before Christmas, I called Hank at the office. I wanted to discuss an idea brewing in my mind. To honor Mrs. Martha Parsons on her hundredth birthday. She was only ninety-five years at the time, but I suggested looking down the road. Down Tripp Street. We would celebrate Mrs. Parsons's birthday by planting daffodils, impatiens, chrysanthemums, and Norway pines in every pothole on Tripp Street. A plant for all seasons. Like Mrs. Martha Parsons. The Mrs. Martha Parsons Tribute Boulevard would solve our pothole problem and garner the approval of the Garden Club.

To solicit support I called Hank. He was in his car at the time, driving home from New Jersey. He had a car phone, but near the Meadowlands it hit a dead spot (between the thirty-yard line and the twenty-yard line to be exact), and we were cut off. He called back, but at a crucial point in our discussion (a debate over whether to plant white or pink impatiens) he disappeared into the Lincoln Tunnel. So did our connection. I ran out of patience as Hank hit another dead spot on the West Side Highway. That's when I suggested he stop by, have a drink, and we could talk in person. But Hank insisted we could cover all matters by phone—my rotary phone and his car phone. Anyway, he was caught in a gridlock on the Hutchinson River Parkway. The road had iced over and traffic wasn't moving. "Dan, now we can really chat." I apologized and explained I couldn't talk because Garth was on call waiting. Garth wanted to tell me he would fax his decision on impatiens colors.

"You should have it in your office tomorrow, Dan."

"Garth," I yelled, "I can't wait. Come on over and we can discuss the project in person. I think Hank's stopping by." But Garth didn't have time. Newmark and Lewis had a sale on car phones, and he wanted one for his second car and the tractor. "Can't you see me plowing snow and talking to the office?"

By the time I gave Garth my office fax number, Hank had arrived at his home. "Sorry, Dan, no time to stop over. I have to program the VCR for a Giants game and Bill Moyers. And Suzie's beeping." Suzie, Hank's hairy dachshund, had ventured outside and was lost in a snowpile. Fortunately she wore an electronic beeper permitting Hank to track her down. "Don't worry, Dan, I have a compact portable phone, and while I'm looking for Suzie we'll talk."

True to his word, Hank called me on the portable phone, but while we were talking he slipped and dropped the phone in the fresh snow. The next sound I heard was a "yip, yip, yip." At least we had found Suzie.

The following morning I raced to the office to read Garth's fax. "Pink impatiens." What a way to start the morning. "Pink impatiens." And then I had my inspiration. Human Contact Day. One day set aside at that time of year when we need contact most. When the fax, the phone, or the beeper is not sufficient. One day. Or maybe every day.

I called Hank. Faxed Garth. Beeped Suzie. "Come to my home Saturday, December 23, at 5:00 P.M. as we celebrate the First Annual Tripp Street Human Contact Day." The response warmed my heart on that cold December day. Soon the entire street was calling to accept my invitation, although certain neighbors were amazed that I answered my own phone. "Don't you have an answering machine?" Garth asked. After three or four similar comments Old Luke called and I replied, "This is 661-4321. I apologize. Our answering machine is not in service. You are talking to a real person." Old Luke was thrilled. "Just like Granddaddy's day!" he exclaimed.

When Human Contact Day arrived, Marion baked a carrot cake in the shape of a phone; I put out a Godiva chocolate bar molded into a fax machine. We wanted to make our guests feel comfortable.

At 5:00 P.M. Hank, Garth, and Suzie gathered on my front porch, where Old Luke searched them for any cellular phones or portable fax machines they might be carrying. Suzie balked and barked when asked for her beeper but we sent her off to play with Teddy. Then the Mrs. Martha Parsons Hundredth Birthday Committee settled down for a winter talk about impatiens. Although we were old friends, the lack of recent personal contact inhibited conversation. Whenever Hank spoke, he put his hand to his ear, as if holding a portable phone; and Garth fed an imaginary roll of fax paper into the space between the seat cushions. My phone rang and I heard Old Luke carrying on a conversation with a computerized recording selling ten pounds of prime Colorado beef with a year's supply of free insurance thrown in. But eventually I invoked the name of Mrs. Martha Parsons and everyone relaxed. Everyone except Teddy, who had swallowed Suzie's beeper and was clearly upset by the strange sounds coming out of her stomach.

Three hours later our mellow gathering was still debating pink versus white impatiens, but a warmth had settled over the room. Even the menorah, the candelabra I had lit for Hanukkah, burned a little brighter than before, and the star atop Otto's Christmas tree was turned on for the first time that holiday season. Yes, human contact had brought light to Tripp Street. The light that is kindled when we are with friends talking about pink and white impatiens. Or not talking. Just being. Together. On a cold, dark day in any season.

9. The Dogwood

How do I record the seasons? By reading the dogwood tree, a white dogwood outside the bedroom window. In April white flowers ripple with awakenings, then blend into the rich green of summer leaves. On a gray October day the nuthatch plucks red berries, and a squirrel scampers along the branches storing food. January. The wind chimes ring and ice sparkles in the winter sun. The dogwood creaks under the weight of frost. How many generations have looked out the bedroom window at the dogwood brushing against the house? Generations experiencing their own change of season. Infants growing into the fullness of their lives. A mother's blond hair streaked with gray.

Each morning when I awaken, my eye pays homage to the dogwood and I affirm my place on time's continuum. As my father did before me, although he did not take his sounding from a dogwood tree. My father was born a century ago in inner-city Baltimore. When he looked out the bedroom window of the Baltimore Hebrew Orphan Asylum, he saw a brick wall. The Baltimore Umbrella Factory. But there was a message on that wall, a message about time and the use of time.

Dad didn't always live next door to the Baltimore Umbrella Factory. He was placed there after the infamous sour-ball raid. Dad told me the story when I was seventeen and he was fifty-seven. In the final days of his life.

. . .

"Son"—a sparrow stole a red berry from the mountain ash as my father sat up in bed—"Son, your grandmother was very poor. Widowed when I was an infant, her dream of a golden land faded into the bland color of the beans we ate every night for dinner. Lentil stew, bean soup, cold beans. I haven't looked at a bean since. So when old Mr. Hauptmann approached my mother with an offer, how could she refuse?"

My father had returned to Baltimore. The year was 1906.

" 'Mary,' Mr. Hauptmann said. 'My candy store. Best bon-bons in town. Women come in from Park Heights, the rich ones with peacock feathers in their hats. And the children, do they love the licorice! Hauptmann Licorice. Best in all Baltimore. Well, Mary, I'm too old to run the store. It's yours. Even has a fresh supply of sour balls. Pay me off slowly. What do you say?' "

Dad smiled, then continued his story.

"How could my mother, your grandmother, refuse? Over the broken window in front of the store she taped a cardboard sign, "Mary's Candee Stor." She was in business.

"Business went pretty well for a month or two. She made a payment to Hauptmann, bought a patch for Dave's pants, new shoes for Ida. Then one day mother caught the flu. Couldn't go to work. She called us into her bedroom.

" 'Children, do Mother a favor. Run the candy store for the day. It's Saturday. I have to open.' "

"Ida, Morris, Dave, Sarah, and me running down Liberty Heights Avenue, over the trolley tracks. A day in a candy store. America was the land where dreams come true. Ida hit the sour balls first. The red ones. Morris de-bonned the bon-bons, and soon it was all over but the vomiting. We didn't have a *Guinness Book of World Records*, but I'd say five children emptying a candy store in half an hour would rate serious consideration.

"Mother didn't find out until she went back to work next day. She never said a word to us. I suppose she thought the candy store raid made up for the thousands of beans we had eaten through the years. But a day later "Mary's Candee Stor" sign was replaced with a new sign. "Clozed."

"Then our mother gathered us in the living room of the clapboard house on Asquith Street.

" 'Children, I can't feed you. Morris, Dave, you're the old-est. I want you to go to the orphanage. You'll eat well. And I'll visit on weekends.' "

I frowned as my father spoke. "Son, many immigrant chil-dren had to live in an orphanage. We were poor. Very poor."

Dad continued. "Anyway, Morris ran away. So my mother sat me down in the overstuffed chair under a picture of my father, his black mustache hanging down to the edge of the picture frame. 'Sammy, would you try the orphanage? If it doesn't work you can come home.'

"My first night at the orphanage was hard. Very hard. Even with Dave in the next bed."

My father paused.

"I stayed in the orphanage for about six years until one day the scholar Dr. Rosenau visited.

" 'Sam, I'd like to send you to Cincinnati. To college. Make something of you.' "

" 'But, Dr. Rosenau, what if I don't make it? I'm just a poor kid from East Baltimore. No one I know has gone to college. Or even left Baltimore.' "

" 'It doesn't matter where you come from. Your neighborhood. Your family. If you've got it in you, you'll make it.' "

"Those were Dr. Rosenau's words, but I wasn't looking at him," my father continued. "I was staring at the motto of the Baltimore Umbrella Factory painted on the red brick wall outside my window, the words I saw every morning. But this time the words took on a different meaning, and I realized wherever I went I would be all right. I would make it. Turning back to Dr. Rosenau, I said, 'I'm ready, sir. When do I leave?' "

Dad sighed, exhausted from speaking.

"You know the rest, son. I've lived in Cincinnati, Cambridge, Heidelberg, Wilkes-Barre, and now Albany. And each move has been more exciting. When the call comes I'm ready. Even for this next journey. Even for this next journey." My father's voice trailed off.

"Dad, you said the words on the brick wall of the umbrella factory gave you the strength to accept each move. But you never told me what the words were."

My father smiled. "You're right, son. The words? 'Baltimore Umbrella Factory. Made in Baltimore and Raised Everywhere!' These were the words I would carry with me. 'Made in Baltimore and Raised Everywhere.' They seemed to say, like the umbrella, if we are open to our world, then we can make it through the years. Anywhere."

And with that my father closed his eyes.

· · ·

As I set down these thoughts, the dogwood tree stands bare. It is winter. Soon the buds will open once again. We will move into a brighter season laced with white petals. Then I will remember the distant words: "Made in Baltimore and Raised Everywhere." And I will be open to the challenge of the seasons. Wherever they may lead.

10. Leatrice Lindburgh

❧

We have two types of people on Tripp Street. The Leatrice Lindburghs and the Brians.

How do they differ? Well, Leatrice Lindburgh, all 250 pounds of her, is an optimist. Brian? He occupies the Chair of Despair and Hopeless Studies at the State University. And if you really want to know the difference between Leatrice and Brian, listen in on a conversation when Brian, dressed in a Shetland sweater and frown, stopped by to visit Leatrice.

"The cold weather's going to kill your fruit trees, Lea. They can't take it."

"Now, Brian"—and Leatrice gave one of her peaches-and-cream smiles—"if it stays cold the freeze might kill the fruit trees but it will also kill the bugs. And Lord knows, we have too many bugs on Tripp Street. Lord knows."

THE DIRT FROM TRIPP STREET

Whether or not the Lord, stressed out managing a vast universe, knows how many bugs we have on Tripp Street remains open to speculation. The Lord does know that every street with a Brian also needs a Leatrice.

The true nature of Leatrice Lindburgh emerged several years ago when the city fathers (and two mothers) decided to divide our town. The original subdivision in 1791 of North Castle into North Castle and New Castle seemed dated. The two towns sprawled over the hillsides, and the authorities voted for a minor redistricting. How were we affected? Heron Pond, previously split between two towns, together with a handful of New Castle homes, was bumped south to North Castle. Leatrice Lindburgh was one of those bumps. On Monday she lived in New Castle. On Tuesday, in North Castle.

For students of geography such minor redistricting might appear insignificant. But old-time residents compare redistricting with the Cuddles Incident. (Cuddles was the Old English sheepdog who bit the Tripp Street mailman on Pearl Harbor Day, relegating Pearl Harbor to page two of the evening newspaper. Page one featured an eight-column picture of Cuddles and an extensive bio.) With redistricting we again made headlines. Reporters converged on Tripp Street. CNN dispensed with normal broadcasting and rushed all available news staff to Tripp Street. NBC canceled Super Bowl coverage, and four reporters and photographers from the *Tokyo Star* caught the first JAL flight from Japan.

When the gaggle of reporters interviewed the Tripp Street residents, they discovered valid opposition to the redistricting plan.

> Lila: *"I object because."*
> Max: *"How can you even ask? The nerve."*
> Vinny: *"Why do I object? Why do I object? Why?"*

Finally the news media interviewed Leatrice Lindburgh, who was busy baking chocolate chip cookies for Jason, Emily, and the neighborhood children. Leatrice insisted the reporters taste her cookies. "How can you ask questions on an empty stomach? Eat, my dears. Eat." Then she settled into her couch, smoothed down her silver hair, and, munching a cookie, faced the cameras.

"This is Channel Seven, and we are in the home of Mrs. Leatrice Lindburgh. Mrs. Lindburgh, would you please give us your opinion?"

Leatrice hesitated, then spoke carefully. "I believe I could have used more chocolate chips, but for the most part this batch of cookies compares favorably with the ones I made for my nieces Suzy and Jennifer. Would you like to see a picture of the twins?"

Channel 7 quickly switched to the studio for a Bud Light commercial while their field reporters briefed Leatrice on the purpose of their visit. "Mrs. Lindburgh, we are here to talk about redistricting. Please keep to the subject."

Leatrice blushed slightly, and once again the cameras rolled.

"We are back with Mrs. Leatrice Lindburgh to discuss redistricting. Madam, would you give us your reaction?"

Leatrice beamed. "Well, I just love being redistricted! It's too, too exciting for someone who never traveled. My husband's family, the Lionel Lindburghs, flew all over the world. Even to Westchester Airport. But not me. At least not until now. Can you imagine? I'm going to be in a new town. And never leave my house. Like Dorothy. 'Somewhere over the rainbow/Bluebirds fly./Birds fly over the rainbow./Now, heaven knows, so do I.' " Leatrice Lindburgh's mellow voice was beamed by satellite from New York to Nairobi.

But Leatrice hadn't finished. "There's another reason I'm overjoyed about being redistricted to North Castle. As you know, New Castle is north of North Castle. Because of this, New Castle always had frightful winters. Even their side of

Heron Pond froze first. Now that I'm in North Castle, maybe the winters will be warmer!"

Channel 7's coverage of Tripp Street brought the station the highest ratings in seventeen years. Leatrice was offered a six-figure contract, which she turned down, content to stay on Tripp Street, where despite redistricting the freezing pattern of Heron Pond has not changed. But North Castle or New Castle, every street needs a Leatrice to warm the heart, buoy up the spirit, and redistrict attitude. Every street and every person.

11. Groundhog Day

────⊙────

At 3:00 A.M. on February 2, the sound of Teddy's barking awakened me from a deep sleep. Outside the house a terrible thrashing could be heard from the garden shed. Following Teddy across the moon-bathed snow, we found the Hav-a-Heart trap I forgot to bring in for the winter. And in the trap was my archenemy the woodchuck, alias groundhog. After twenty years of losing my gardens to groundhogs I had an opportunity for revenge. Groundhog, how shall I kill you? Let me count the ways. Hire the pit bull and Doberman who live across the road? Tie peach pits to your legs and dump you in Heron Pond? Bind you with the cucumber vines you pulled off my trellis last August? I consider myself a gentle man, but disposing of a woodchuck filled me with joy. Yes, God is just. Eventually the good are rewarded, the evil punished. "Groundhog, in the morning you will have one wish before sentencing is carried out. One last meal left over from the garden. A tomato, string beans (cooked any way you desire), a squash. Think well, wood-chuck, think well." Leaving the captive, I returned to the house, slipped under the quilt, and told Marion of our night visitor.

"What's a groundhog doing out in the depths of winter?" she asked. "Groundhogs hibernate—unless, unless." The bed glowed with the warmth of Marion's inspiration. "Well?" I sighed, ready to go to sleep. "Unless," Marion continued, "we have a special groundhog?"

"Marion, what could be special about a groundhog? Go to sleep."

But Marion was burrowing into the groundhog mystery.

"Did it have grizzled brownish fur, short legs, a heavyset body?"

"Marion, this is ridiculous. All groundhogs fit that descrip-tion!"

Marion, deep into a secret tunnel, refused to let up. "Did it have a nametag around the neck?"

"A nametag? A nametag?"

"Exactly. Go back out and see if the woodchuck has a nametag."

"Marion!"

"No, I'm serious." And as Marion always does when she is serious, she yanked the quilt off my body, leaving me exposed to a freezing February night.

"Okay, okay, I'll go." And we were off. Teddy and me. The things one does for a piece of quilt. This time, however, as we approached the Hav-a-Heart trap, the groundhog curled up in one corner whimpering, and Teddy, moved to pity, gave the groundhog a Kibbles and Nibbles dog bone. Then I saw it—the nametag. Phil. In large bold letters. And in fine print: "If found please return to Punxsutawney." I rushed back to the bedroom and announced, "Marion, we have Punxsutawney Phil sleeping over. The groundhog that tells the weather!" Marion gave me one of her "I told you so" smiles and scolded me. "Tomorrow's Groundhog Day, and Phil's a long way away from home. He's still got promises to keep and miles to go before he sleeps, and the poor thing's caught in our Hav-a-Heart trap! Quick, let him out."

But I wasn't so eager. Weather prediction always fascinated me. Not the sophisticated meteorologist forecasts but the folksy predictions. For instance: *Old Farmer's Almanac;* katydids; the yellow tones of the willow trees; Punxsutawney Phil. "Marion, I'm going to keep Phil. Since 1898, Phil's ancestors have broadcast from the Punxsutawney Club or the Slumbering Groundhog lodge in Quarryville, Pennsylvania, but this year Groundhog Day will be celebrated on Tripp Street."

Marion was shocked. "What has happened to your sense of ethics? The pledge you made at the seminary. Kidnapping Phil is wrong." And for the second time in one night she yanked off the quilt.

Usually appeals to a code of ethics touch my professional conscience. Not this time. However, to appease Marion, relieve guilt, and retrieve quilt, I promised to fax Phil's prediction to Punxsutawney first thing in the morning.

At 6:00 A.M. I dressed in my top hat and frock coat (the required dress at the Punxsutawney Club) and, joined by Teddy, Marion, and little Jason from up the street, marched out to the Hav-a-Heart trap singing the traditional Groundhog song:

> *Glory! Glory! to the groundhog.*
> *Glory! Glory! to the groundhog.*
> *Glory! Glory! to the groundhog.*
> *Today the prophet comes.*

Phil perked up when he heard the Groundhog Day chorus. He stood on his rear paws, puffed out his chest, and looked very much like Bob, the meteorologist on the morning news. There was no doubt that God created groundhogs to forecast weather. In fact, maybe, just maybe, groundhogs destroy gardens because of frustration. What satisfaction can a groundhog gain from a single day's employment as a weatherman?

The sun rose over Crooks Notch when I lifted Phil out of his cage. Would he see his shadow? Would spring be slow in coming? Carefully I lowered Phil to the ground. "Okay, Phil, forecast!" Phil turned up his lips in a smile revealing white woodchuck teeth and then went to work, wobbling out to the middle of the sunlit lawn. He turned to the north, and there was his shadow. Then, with an apologetic shrug, Phil returned to his cage. It would be a long winter. Six more weeks.

Later that morning as I watched the news and learned of the nationwide search for Phil, who for the first time in 150 years failed to appear at Punxsutawney, I reviewed the strange phenomenon of Groundhog Day. Why, on a sunny day, when the world radiates cheer, did winter receive a six-week extension? After many days of pondering this matter I concluded that Phil possessed a uniquely human quality. On that sunny day Phil stood in his own light, and if you stand in your own sunlight, of course you create shadows—for yourself and for your world. Poor Phil, you brought your own winter because you stood in your own way! You were your own worst enemy. What a shame, when spring waits just around the corner. Poor Phil. Poor Punxsutawney Phil.

12. The "S" Words

Why did God create snow? A theologian with a Ph.D. in linguistics once explained that when God created the world He ended up with a surplus of words still knocking around in the "S" bin: slush, skating, skiing, slippery, sanders, shivering. Searching for a generic "S" word to cover all of the above, God created SNOW!

Possible. But there's a second theory. On a gloomy winter afternoon, Teddy and I went walking on Tripp Street. The grass, brown from winter, revealed bare spots, and the road was muddy. Otto's evergreens, stripped by deer, displayed tufts of brown needles, and a Valvoline container lay on the lawn. Earlier in the month a car dumped two tires and a rusty fender in the gully near Garth's house, and since Monday was garbage day, plastic bags lined the driveways. All in all, Tripp Street presented an ugly face to the world.

Then God went to work, via "Accurate Oscar" Weatherfield the meteorologist on television's "Weather or Not." Oscar huffed and he puffed and his chest heaved under a tartan plaid vest. "Good evening, good folks. Tonight the temperature will hover between forty-four and forty-five degrees with a seven and a half percent chance of rain at one-fifteen A.M. Monday will be sunny and warm."

Monday morning dawned with eight inches of snow already on the ground and a revised prediction of a four-inch additional accumulation. "Sorry, folks"—Oscar grinned—"the air traffic controllers missed the cold front in the Canadian Rockies, which collided with a storm system from the south. But have a good day. This is Accurate Oscar Weatherfield signing off until tomorrow."

Good old Oscar. When God detects cockiness among his earthly family, a sense that we have control over our world, God flies Oscar in to create a little turbulence. The snowstorm blew out to sea in late morning, leaving Tripp Street bathed in white. The jagged points of the picket fence were soft and fluffy, the rusty metal garbage cans stood like snowmen. Even the Valvoline can had vanished beneath God's wonderful whitewashed world. Teddy and I sat by the window hypnotized by snowy innocence. Teddy broke the spell by scratching on the kitchen door. Necessity over beauty. The dog raced outside leaving, among other droppings, her paw prints on the snow. Then Otto glided by on cross-country skis, his tracks intersecting Teddy's design. And there was Lila with little Emily. The child watched as her mother hopped on the right side of the sugar maple on one foot, then on the left side with the other foot. "Mother!" Emily giggled. "It's a miracle! You walked through the tree!" Teddy, Otto, and Lila had placed a fresh imprint on the day.

The heavy treads of the snowplow strained up Murphy's Hill swoosh-swooshing sand on the road, and the garbage truck left black cleat marks on our packed driveway. By evening a splotchy quilt reappeared on the front lawn and the Valvoline container poked its greasy head above the surface. Tripp Street returned to normal. But for a few hours in late morning we had been pure and white—a clean landscape glistening in the morning sun. Willing to accept any design we wished to etch on the face of the earth.

And as I remembered the winter snow, I mused. If only we could understand that each new morning holds the crystal flakes of promise. Even without a snowstorm. If only. But in case we forget, just in case we forget . . .

That's why God created snow.

13. The Day of the Blizzard

'Twas the night of the blizzard,
And all through the house,
Not a creature was stirring,
Not even a mouse.
Then out on the driveway
I heard a great sound,
Max's Giant Brown Reindeer
Pulling a snowplow around.

Max had plowed driveways on Tripp Street since 1946. Or was it 1947? Some say Max appeared with God's very first snowfall, but that would be before 1946. Of course Max didn't have reindeer or even a snowplow. He owned a rusty old pickup with a bent blade on the front that pushed the snow in swiggles and swaggles. Max's plow was snow-friendly and pebble-friendly. By springtime, when the piles of snow lining the drive-way melted, most of the gravel from the driveway was on the grass mulching the daffodils.

We never complained. Raking pebbles off the lawn builds fortitude, and everyone on the block, all Max's customers, set aside one day to rake. Put our driveways back in shape. Before I moved to Tripp Street, Rake Day occurred on the second Sunday in April, but in recent years Rake Day fell on the first Monday after the second Tuesday in April, permitting one more of those three-day holidays. Memorial Day, Labor Day, and Rake Day. A trio of patriotic holidays. We even had a flag that we hoisted on the street sign—a mud-brown background with the image of a red rake. And the Tripp Street chorus of happy rakers raised their voices in tribute to Rake Day.

> *Hi-ho, hi-ho, a-raking I will go.*
> *After the snow, after the snow, a-raking I will go.*

Then Max would honk the horn of his Ford pickup, and we would pledge our allegiance to the rake, to Max, and to winters still to come.

Max never charged for snowplowing. Sure, we usually left a little money in his mailbox at the far end of Tripp Street, or Marion would bake a cake with white icing symbolic of snow and black jelly beans to represent pebbles. But Max never charged. He was a Tripp Streeter, committed to using all available resources to assist his neighbors.

> *I am a Tripp Streeter, O don't you see,*
> *I remove snow without a fee.*

Max approached snow removal philosophically. Often when we would sit and discuss great philosophers like Plato, Kant, and Charlie Brown, Max would suggest, "Those thinkers, they dreamed of ideal societies, but me, I have only one goal in life—to clear snow. To help a Volvo, Toyota, Chevrolet move into the present with traction." And whenever I heard Max's mellifluous words I felt a sudden surge of inspiration. Ah, Max, what a wonderful world this would be if we could progress forward with traction, skidding neither to right or left. Secure. Our rubber treads gripping the scattered pebbles of our life.

At the age of eighty-four two events forced Max to abandon his mission of sending Tripp Streeters out of their driveways into daily life. First, most people on Tripp Street paved their driveways, effectively eliminating the real fun of snowplowing—pushing pebbles. Second, on a routine November preseason run Max's Ford pickup dropped its motor into a giant pothole. For a while Max lamented the demise of his raison d'être, but on a bitterly cold December day as I jogged past Max's house I spied a Rapid Sno Removal truck unloading a carton onto his driveway. Max, dressed in a black suit, his best beret, with a carefully groomed white mustache, rushed out. "Dan, I'm back in business. Just bought a new snowplow. Best model Rapid Sno makes. The Whoosher."

I was happy for Max. How many of us will have the confidence at eighty-four to begin again? With a Whoosher no less. And yet, hadn't Max reached retirement age? Wasn't he entitled to sit in his rocking chair, smoke his old pipe, and watch young Vinny plow our driveways? "Max," I suggested, "you've cleared enough driveways for one life. With or without a Whoosher. You've outlived plow, pickup, and pebbles. Do you really want to clean driveways and push against the drifts of time? Reconsider. Return the Whoosher."

Max grinned. "Dan, the Whoosher's not for driveways. No, I am willing to hand over my driveways to Vinny. But since I was a child I had a dream, and this Whoosher will help me reach that dream."

"A dream? What kind of dream?"

But Max refused to answer. "Wait, Dan. Wait for the first snowfall."

I didn't have long to wait. Winter came early that year. A cold winter. The beginning of December averaged eighteen degrees, and children skated on the frozen ponds of northern Westchester. The first snow arrived on a Tuesday in midmorning. Schools dismissed early and offices closed at 3:00 P.M. Children made snowmen and I brought in logs for the fireplace. By evening seven or eight inches of snow had fallen.

Next morning, life returned to normal. Vinny plowed the driveway and I walked up Tripp Street to visit with Max, but he wasn't home. Sarah, his wife, pointed up the street. "He's there, at Heron Pond. You know that dream of his?" As I approached Heron Pond, I heard the whoosh-whoosh of Max's Whoosher and saw him standing in the middle of Heron Pond wearing black rubber galoshes. The old kind with the snaps that never snap. Snow flew in every direction, and Max's mini-blizzard had already cleared half the pond. When he saw me, Max turned off the motor, removed his fuzzy earmuffs, and gently caressed the steel handle of the snowblower. "Everything it's supposed to be" was all Max said. "Everything."

"So, Max, this was your dream? Since you were a kid? To clean ponds? I don't get it."

Max sat down on the Whoosher. I pulled over a log and joined him.

"To clean ponds? Not exactly, Dan. But when I was a child I loved to skate. I'd sit in school and dream of skating. Soon as the final bell rang I'd run home, grab a handful of chocolate chip cookies and my skates, and head for the pond. Round Pond. Don't know why they called it Round Pond. Looked more like a finger."

Max was quiet. I had lost him to a time seventy-five years ago. He had returned home. To his childhood. The one home we take with us wherever we go.

"Max? Max? You were saying."

"Right. Well, anyway, I'd run to Round Pond, roll down the bank and slip into my skates. But usually the pond was covered with snow. I couldn't skate. Sometimes on the week-ends a father would shovel off a little circle of ice, but during the week? All the dads were at work. I remember sitting by Round Pond imagining the clear ice hiding under the snow, waiting for me, but I couldn't get to it. What a waste! So I'd go back home, sit by the wood-burning stove, and fancy I was doing figure eights, skating backwards, gliding for miles and miles, even though Round Pond only went a few hundred yards. That's when I made a vow. 'Max,' I said to myself, 'when you're big, like Papa, you're going to clear ponds for children. Now don't forget, Max.' Well, I didn't forget, but I never had the time. Too many driveways, too many pebbles."

We smiled, remembering Rake Day.

Max went on. "Now I have the time. Don't know how many years I'll still be around, but I have the time and I have my Whoosher. And I'm going to use my last years snowblowing for the kids. Give those children daydreaming in school something to look forward to. Then after I'm gone, maybe they'll say, 'Good old Max, he used the twilight of his years to put a new generation on ice.' Doesn't have to be so flowery of course."

In late afternoon Jason tottered out on the blades of his skates, and Emily appeared from the modern gray house. Soon the Culligan boys from Greenwood Place lit a fire along the shore, and Heron Pond filled with the laughter of children skating on clear ice, clear enough to catch the last reflections of a December sun fading behind a hemlock.

And in the distant shadows of Heron Pond an old man in galoshes and furry earmuffs leaned on his shiny red Whoosher. Watching. Round Pond had come full circle.

Spring

14. Tripp Street Pothole Association

---⟨❧⟩---

"**M**y good friends, welcome to the annual meeting of the TSPA." Otto's voice reverberated through the living room of his contemporary home where the art of Warhol, Nevelson, and Rauschenberg lined the walls. Otto was also an artist. In front of the fireplace he displayed his latest work, "Still Life with Tailpipe," a massive metal sculpture made of tailpipes, mufflers, and an occasional catalytic converter. Where had Otto acquired these automobile artifacts? From the three score potholes and ten pockmarking Tripp Street. Potholes snaring cars' undergarments.

Otto continued: "This year, as in years past, the TSPA, Tripp Street Pothole Association, has convened to discuss a motion for repairs made by Dr. Lydia Schultz." Lydia, a dentist of some repute, could not swallow the concept of cavities, even in a street; and since she moved to Tripp Street four years ago she had campaigned for fixing the potholes. Her first attempt, chronicled in the *Tripp Street Chronicles* under the chapter entitled "Pothole Potpourri," describes the meeting. "Dr. Lydia B. Schultz appeared wearing a macadam-colored T-shirt with the imprint 'Fill in, Don't Fall in.' Local residents wore mauve T-shirts bearing the motto 'Tripp Street Is Just a Bowl of Potholes.' Old Luke spoke on behalf of the TSPA, reminding Dr. Schultz that in the early days, when the road was dirt, an entire car might disappear after a washout. 'We've come a long way!' Old Luke concluded. Unimpressed, Dr. Schultz, in an impassioned plea, argued for fixing all life's imperfections. Of course her motion to repave was voted down." (*Tripp Street Chronicles,* May 1988.)

Lydia's proposal, submitted in 1989 and 1990, gained only one vote, but last year Dr. Schultz brought her entire family to the meeting. Aunts, uncles, nephews, cousins. Some from as far away as Chappaqua. Caught by surprise, the TSPA admitted defeat and agreed to repave.

I still remember.

A pungent smell of burning tar drifted into open windows the week they paved Tripp Street. Even the smell of broccoli from Marion's vegetarian dinner retreated before the onslaught of tar. Unable to drive on Tripp Street, I parked below on Heather Place and followed the deer paths home. Only Teddy ventured onto the wet tar, leaving her mark for all time. Finally the Highway Department finished the last stretch and left us with a beautifully manicured street. Lydia beamed and suggested we clean the street weekly with fluoride. "We'll avoid future potholes." Since our budget was now deeply in the hole, we rejected this plan. We did assess the residents $1.50 per person for a new street sign: "Welcome to Tripp Street. The Empire State's Most Beautiful Pavement." And it was. Until the winter, when an onslaught of freezes and thaws caused the road to buckle and crack. Even one of Lydia's porcelain bridges couldn't keep Tripp Street together again. We had re-entered the pothole era.

At this year's meeting in Otto's house, Tripp Streeters gloated over their victory. When Lydia entered, smug faces beamed with an "I told you so" look. "Who were you to tamper with tradition?" And when the brakes of a Trans Am screeched at old Number 93 (the car-busting pothole at 93 Tripp Street), I shrank into my seat as my neighbors cheered for the pothole. Of course Lydia again made an impassioned plea for repairing (minus the support of her family, who had defected to other worthwhile causes). But Lydia's case was hopeless.

Leaving the meeting, I caught up to her in front of "Still Life with Tailpipe."

"Lydia, please don't take it personally. I agree. A street without potholes would be better, but you are asking for the impossible. We live in an imperfect world, and if you can't fill in the imperfections learn to navigate around them. That's a greater challenge."

I believe my words touched Lydia, because she flashed me a giant smile, exposing pearly white teeth. Except I think I detected a small cavity in a left incisor.

15. A Stone Wall

~~~᷼~~~

We really didn't need another stone wall on our property. Stone walls already encircled the house, and even the driveway, once a cow run, had a neat border of stones. But I decided to build a stone wall in the only area of my property still wall-less. The front porch. I was aware of Robert Frost's words of caution:

> *Before I built a wall I'd ask to know*
> *What I was walling in or walling out.*

What was I walling in or walling out? On my front porch? Nothing. Absolutely nothing. But my muse came from an older poet, William Shakespeare:

THE DIRT FROM TRIPP STREET

And this our life, exempt from public haunt,
Finds tongues in trees, books in the running brooks,
Sermons in stones . . . [As You Like It, Act II, Scene 1]

It was the phrase "Sermons in stones" that sparked my building plans. I was desperately in need of sermons for the holy days and ready to look anywhere. Even the crevices of a stone wall.

How do you build a wall? After extensive research in the library I found an easy-to-apply recipe. "To build a wall, first find a stone." Digging my garden convinced me that our yard was a storehouse of stones, but moving the stones proved to be too much of a challenge. In vain I searched Robert Frost and William Shakespeare for inspiration. Only that great psychological treatise *The Little Engine That Could* offered constructive advice. The Little Engine said, "Believe in yourself, believe in yourself." So each morning while brushing my teeth I repeated over and over, "I think I can, I think I can. I thought I could, I thought I could." But I couldn't!

In the old days, when Asa Sheldon, the author of *Yankee Drover; Being the Unpretending Life of Asa Sheldon, Farmer, Trader and Working Man, 1788–1870,* built stone walls he used oxen. Sheldon wrote, "I found one good yoke of oxen would slip along with five tons comfortably." My stones only weighed seventy to eighty pounds, but if I had some oxen . . . So I set off on a house-to-house hunt for oxen. Otto had a Doberman pinscher, Lydia a bowl of guppies, Max a stone elephant sitting on his patio, and Garth had his collection of Jaguars, Cougars, Broncos, and Colts. But no one had a yoke of oxen. Reduced to manual labor and small stones, I spent a long weekend moving stones, and by Tuesday morning my porch resembled a quarry.

Unfortunately, I neglected to leave room for my wall. So the next day I rolled the stones off the porch onto the front lawn. Rocks sprawled along the path, under the walnut tree, and leaned against the dogwood. Ever since Teddy had claimed the front lawn as a burial site for bones, we were excluded from the annual Garden Club Tour; a yard filled with stones sealed the verdict. Marion, suspicious of my "do it yourself" projects, feared for the future of our lawn. I assured her the pristine green of crabgrass would soon return, although I agreed the lawn had the appearance of chaos.

Before laying the foundation stone, I studied local walls, like those of John Matthews, "Waller John," who lived in the 1860s, when our house was built. Even with my research I soon discovered that building walls is a distinct art, one I had not completely mastered. Utilizing the Tower of Babel principle, I piled rock upon rock, defying the forces of gravity, until the pile cascaded onto the pachysandra, and I found myself babbling. But gradually I mastered wall building. I found 3:00 A.M. an especially productive period. At that hour visions appeared of proper rock placement, and I descended to my floodlit porch to shift a rock or fill a chink. Occasionally I took a stone back to my bed for further study. But still, not a sermon in stone. And Marion had run out of patience. "When will you clean the stones off the front lawn? Our grounds are a disgrace."

Days passed into weeks. The wall was rising. Although Teddy could easily step over the wall, I noticed chipmunks could no longer jump it and scurried around the ends. On May 24, at 3:33 P.M., I topped the wall with a capping stone. Finished. A wall of beauty is a joy forever, and this wall was a masterpiece. Four feet long from end to end, eight and a half inches high. When Marion drove in that evening, I took her by the hand, led her to the wall, and pointed. "Oh, Dan," she said. "Oh, Dan." That was all she said. Not even an exclamation mark. But then she looked out on the lawn and from the depths of her heart exclaimed, "Oh, Dan, you finally cleared those awful stones off the lawn! You have made order out of chaos." Modestly I stepped back, realizing I was part of an outstanding tradition. Hadn't God done the same thing? In the beginning the world was without form. Then God got busy creating heaven and earth, and before you could say, "Cosmic significance," we were in excellent shape. Of course God worked faster, but since that time each one of us accepts the challenge to place order on the world. At least a small part of the world. Like the front lawn.

Inspired by my role in the grand design, I hugged Marion and smiled. "Dear, I'm glad you're happy. Once again the lawn is *As You Like It*." And that is when I knew I had finally found my sermon in stone.

16. I Was Stoned on Tripp Street

I was stoned on Tripp Street.

In the spring spadework began for a garden next to my raspberry patch. To celebrate the first shovelful I tied a yellow zucchini to the old oak tree and welcomed my neighbors. Seedy Old Luke, representing Farmers Then and Now, came dressed in faded blue work shorts, varicose veins sprouting in every direction. Max dropped by to bring greetings from the local chapter of AA, Artichokes Anonymous. Young Emily of Ripe Tomatoes of America wore a highly revealing jumpsuit, but her parents sent her away, nipping in the bud any possible embarrassment. (Garth, always on the lookout for a possible investment of time and energy, let out a scythe of disappointment as Young Emily disappeared.) Even little Jason drove up on his three-wheeler, but when he discovered the only food being served was chocolate-covered Japanese beetles, he pedaled back home. And Lydia's aunt, Lady Bug Ronson, flew in several hundred ladybugs to fight enemy insects. Once again Tripp Street's community feeling had come to the fore.

I invoked God's name—"Lord, please look down on what grows up"—and handed out souvenir spade pins in honor of the day. (It should be noted that Teddy did not appreciate the spade pins. She had endured an operation of similar name the previous day and was still in mourning for future generations of Teddys who would never see the light of day.) Then I changed from my three-piece black suit into designer jeans, cut the ribbon holding the yellow zucchini to the old oak tree, and to a resounding cheer sank my spade into the dirt of Tripp Street. A family of earthworms wiggled away, and a mole, watching me pile up earth, shuddered as I made a mountain out of his molehill.

Work proceeded according to schedule until twenty minutes into the project I encountered rock. Clink. Clink. Clink. Shifting several feet away, I made a test probe only to find more stones. I called up to Marion watching from the porch. "Marion, this yard's full of stones. How am I going to have a garden? It isn't fair." Marion, fearing another one of my half-completed projects, was short on empathy. "Life isn't fair, Dan. It's life." Which sounded like one of my sermons, which was the last thing I wanted to hear at that moment. Whatever the fairness of life, I knew Westchester still bore the residue of the Pleistocene ice age when glaciers passed by and dropped off a massive shipment of stones, enough to build 250,000 miles of stone walls in New England and New York, not counting the enormous surplus still beneath the ground. Yes, Marion, life isn't fair, it's stones. So like generations of farmers before me I set out to remove stones.

I already knew stones were heavy, but if I wanted a garden I would have to move them. Even the large ones. I brought in crowbars, sledgehammers, and muscle power. After three weeks on the Nautilus machine I tackled the stones and lifted several of the fifty-pounders to knee level. That's when my back went out and I met Dr. Schwartz the orthopedist, "Bones" the chiropractor, and Lo Mein the acupuncturist.

I also met Wimpy. Wimpy weighed 133 pounds, stood five foot three, and worked on the building site behind our house, slinging hundred-pound cement bags onto his shoulder with the grace of a ballet dancer. I hired Wimpy to clear my land. After a week he had a twenty-by-thirty-foot patch ready for planting. Then he came to me, his wiry body rippling with enthusiasm. "Dan, why don't I teach you the proper way to lift stones. It's easy." As if in answer a pain shot down my sacroiliac and an inner voice erupted, "Don't you dare say yes, buddy."

"Wimpy, what's the point of my learning?"

"Well, for one thing, Dan, I'm on to another assignment. You're on your own. If you want a garden, you better carry your own weights."

My sacroiliac grimaced, sending another twinge from waist to calf. A heavy load descended on my shoulders. Kerplunk.

"I guess you're right, Wimpy, but I'm not strong enough to lift stones. I tried."

"Nonsense. The trick is how you carry the stones. Technique, Dan, technique." And Wimpy knelt on one knee, gripped a stone, jerked a little here, grunted a little there, and lifted the stone onto his shoulder. "Don't bend over, Dan. You can't carry a hundred pounds when you're bent over. Face that stone, knee first. Try my technique. Try."

I tried. At first nothing happened. "Ugh! Ugh! Ugh!" My grunts echoed through the neighborhood. Wimpy shifted my position slightly. "Everyone carries their burdens in their own way. Find a comfortable position. And cut out those 'Ughs'. It's not you." So I experimented. Right knee forward. Left knee forward. "Agh" instead of "Ugh." "Yuk" instead of "Agh." (Finally settling for "Yugh, yugh, yugh.") To my amazement I lifted a hundred-pound stone. Triumphant, I ran into the house with my stone to show Marion and dropped it on the bed, where unfortunately she was still asleep.

I am now in the third year of carrying stones and am the envy of my neighborhood. Occasionally strangers call: "Dan, will you teach us your method of carrying stones?" My agent wants me to write a self-help book called *The Modified Wimpy Method: A Guide to Carrying Your Burden Through Life*, $11.98. With a pet stone attached. I refused. I will not perpetrate a sham. Everyone has to find his own method of lifting stones. I only know what works for me.

I also know my garden grows. And gone are the days when I was stoned on Tripp Street.

Ugh! Agh! Yuk! Yugh!

17. Run, Rabbi, Run

---©----

"Run, Rabbi, run." "Run, Rabbi, run." "Run, Rabbi, run." The cheer followed me along Route 128, and my chest burst with pride, rippling the red letters emblazoned on my white T-shirt: "Heel and Sole 12K Race." Who was the voice urging me on as I stumbled and fumbled past the halfway mark? Who? Being of a religious nature, I assumed the voice was the voice of God, helping his earthly partner. As the Psalmist said, "My help cometh from the Lord." And did I ever need help! I looked into the heavens and winked. "Thanks, God. Thanks for taking a moment out of your superhuman schedule to look down on a lonely rabbi running the paths of life. Thanks, God." But it wasn't God. No clouds. No thunder. No lightning. No God.

"Run, Rabbi, run." Who? Then I found the voice echoing from the door of Broadway Pizza. A girl's voice. Sally. Sweet

Sally. Munching on a slice of sausage pizza. Sally, winner of the SRR Award in my religious school. "Presented annually to that sixth-grader demonstrating the womanly qualities of Sarah, Rebecca, and Rachel." Yes, it was Sally, dressed as a biblical matriarch in a blue denim jean suit from the Gap, with the letters SRR sewn on the back. "Run, Rabbi, run. You've moved up to fortieth! Run, Rabbi, run." Fortieth. Out of a field of forty-two. For most runners a discouraging position. But for me the fulfillment of a dream. Forty. A religious number. Why? Well, Noah hit dry land after floating for forty days. And Moses. Forty was a winner for Moses. Forty years backpacking in the Sinai. Forty days climbing Mount Sinai. And for those interested in dress styles, forty started it all. When Adam saw Eve naked he giggled, and Eve, embarrassed, but lacking a Bloomingdale's in Eden, fashioned a dress out of forty fig leaves. So the garment industry was born.

Fortieth in the Heel and Sole Race. An enviable number. My chance to join the Fortysomething Club. Be considered for a footnote in the *New Newly Revised Edition of the Bible*. Worth the effort.

Sally's voice faded as I passed Citibank, but withdrawing a second burst of energy, I broke into a chant. A runner's chant.

> *Old Man Daniel,*
> *That Old Man Daniel,*
> *Just keep runnin' along.*
>
> *I gets weary*
> *And sick of tryin'.*
> *I'm tired of runnin'*
> *And feared of dyin',*
> *But Old Man Daniel*
> *He just keeps runnin' along.*
>
> *Me and me, I sweat and strain.*
> *Knees all achin', my back's in pain.*
> *Lift that sole,*

Raise that heel,
Make it to the finish line before you keel.

Old Man Daniel
That Old Man Daniel . . .

I finished fortieth. My personal best after ten years of running. Ten years of huffing and puffing. Looking miserable. Feeling miserable. Telling everyone I felt wonderful. Running
through youth. Running into middle age. Eyes fixed on the
road. No time to stop. No time to look. Run, Rabbi, run!

Then I moved to Tripp Street and ran into disaster. Tripp
Street is a jogger's nightmare. First, there is Murphy's Hill.
Straight up. Higher than a hundred Murphys standing on each
other's shoulders. And curves. Blind curves. Especially near
Hank's house, where Hank backs down his driveway on garbage
day without seeing me jog by. He can't see. His Jaguar's filled
with garbage for the morning pickup. And the pothole outside
Old Luke's house. A real ankle grabber. Old Luke won't part
with his pothole. "Keeps our street rural." When we bought our
house on Tripp Street, I knew my jogging was an endangered
species. Oh! Oh! Oh! My wife, Marion, looked at the street
philosophically. "Life is filled with obstacles." I love jogging,
not philosophy. How would I adjust?

That's when Old Luke shared a drop of Tripp Street lore.
More than a drop. A jug. Very Very Old Luke's jug. Very Very
Old Luke, as previously noted, lived on Tripp Street in the days
of the pig farm and spent his evenings drinking at Willard's
Still. In the early hours of the morning Very Very Tipsy Old
Luke, holding on to trees with his left hand and waving the jug
in his right hand, staggered home. Day after day, night after
night, Old Luke trampled a path up Murphy's Hill until he
arrived at his cabin near the burial site of "Old Sam, He Was
a Good Horse." Eventually the path became Pig Road, then
Tripp Street, although it should have been called Jug's End or
Weaver Street. "That's why Tripp Street has so darn many

curves," Old Luke said. "But sober or drunk, Granddaddy always made it home. He just went at his own pace."

His own pace. And one Saturday as I sat at the peak of Murphy's Hill and observed my neighbors out exercising, I understood what Old Luke meant. Keith, a cross-country runner at Fordham Prep, raced up Murphy's Hill, leaped across the potholes, and glided into the final stretch of his mini-marathon. Ruffles and Truffles, Lydia's golden retrievers, pulled her up the hill faster than she intended; and the Ottos rested on every third boulder. Tripp Streeters mastering the road at their own pace. With or without a jug.

And me? I walk. No more 12K races or the sounds of Sally cheering me on. Now I have entered the second phase of life's marathon, comfortable with my own pace. Even though no one yells, "Walk, Rabbi, walk." No one.

18. Pasang: Some Up Go and Some Down Go

~~~~~~~~~~~~~~~~~~~~~~~~~~~~~~~~~~~~~

What will Pasang say when he visits Murphy's Hill?

Who is Pasang? First let me tell you about Murphy's Hill. According to local legend, when God drew up His master plan for the creation of our town, He miscalculated and ended up with extra dirt. Too much inventory. Shipping costs being high between heaven and earth, God decided to let the excess dirt lie in a heap at the end of Tripp Street. That's how Tripp Street inherited Murphy's Hill. God's leftovers.

On snowy days children toboggan and sleighride on Murphy's Hill. In summer potential car buyers test the power of sleek Buicks, Toyotas, and Mercedes on Murphy's Hill. According to the April 1990 *Murph's Turf and Road* magazine, a Porsche ascended in two minutes and twenty seconds, a Chevy in four minutes and thirty-nine seconds, and a Yugo was pushed up the hill in two hours and forty-five minutes before rolling off the cliff into the gulch on Heather Road.

Murphy's Hill is not for the weak of heart and legs. Occasionally I invite friends for a walk. "Sounds great, Dan. How far?"

"How many miles are we going to walk? Two, three, four?"

"Irrelevant," I reply.

"Irrelevant?"

"Exactly. You see, the trip includes Murphy's Hill, steepest darn hill in the Northeast, and Murphy's Hill can't be measured in miles. Or even in time."

"Come on, Dan. You can tell us how far. Don't be ridiculous. How can you live without knowing how long something takes?"

That's when Pasang, a fourteen-year-old Nepalese boy, enters the conversation. Pasang guided me on a trek in the Himalaya mountains. Wearing a white fisherman's hat, he scampered barefoot up mountain paths carrying four-by-eight-foot wooden planks on his back. He also erased the question "How far?" from my vocabulary.

The day I met Pasang I had already asked "How far?" at least five times. In Kathmandu, before setting off on the trek: "How far do I have to carry my backpack?" On the flight into the Himalaya mountains: "How far away is the landing strip?" This was a question I shouldn't have asked. A weathered old mountain climber seated next to me caressed his scarred walking stick and pointed out the window. A craggy peak loomed directly in front of the plane. I should have asked, "How will we land?" Then my religious nature took over. I prayed. "Prepare to meet thy mountain, O Daniel." The next thing I knew I was on the ground at 8,000 feet! Was it really the ground? Was I alive? Dead? A celestial chorus filled the air: "Freude, Schöner Götterfunken, Tochter aus Elysium." If I were dead, somehow I had ended up in the German-speaking section of heaven! Then another trekker explained. "You're very much alive and that's Beethoven's Ninth Symphony. The final movement. 'Joy, Joy, daughter of Elysium.' " How had the Vienna Chorale made it to the foothills of Everest? Then I caught sight of Pasang plugged into a Sony Walkman, given to him by a trekker Pasang had guided up Mount Everest. The Walkman came with one tape, Beethoven's Ninth.

Pasang tied my big blue duffel on a lumbering yak and offered friendly advice. "Sir, on a narrow path yaks always have the right of way." The young Sherpa slipped into rubber sandals, I laced my hiking boots, and we were off. To Everest. "Pasang, how far to Everest?" Silence. A simpler question. "Pasang, how far do we walk today?" Silence. Probably a communication barrier. I raised my voice. Spoke slowly. *"Pasang. How far do we have to go today?"*

An impish smile spread from one side of his headset to the other. "How far? Do you walk fast? Do you walk slow? How are you on rocks? In mud? Across streams?" Then, as the chorus leaped into Beethoven's grand finale, Pasang fixed me with a look honed on the wisdom of the mountains. "Sir." He paused. I clung to a precipice of expectation. Would I finally have the authoritative answer to the lifelong question "How far?" "Sir, today we have some up go and some down go." That was all he said. "Some up go and some down go." And that was enough.

We climbed. We descended. Down to the dry riverbed, along the rocky bottom, up a cliff in sight of Everest, then across a suspension bridge swinging above the Kosi River. We went at our own speed, from 8,000 up to 11,000 feet, then down to 9,000. Back up to 11,000. Led by yaks and a boy named Pasang.

The moon climbed over the white crown of Everest when I hobbled into camp after the first day of trekking. Sore muscles confirmed the up go and down go, and my left ankle revealed a purple boot imprint. That night I almost asked, "How far did we walk today?" but the urge passed quickly. In fact I've been out of the Himalayas for over a year and I haven't asked, "How far?" Does it matter? Our travels through life are measured by the steepness of the hills we climb and descend, the problems surmounted. The up goes and down goes tell us where we have been, where we are, and where we are going.

Not long ago I heard from Pasang. He wants to visit. See our mountains. So I invited him to Tripp Street. I even bought my own Walkman and a tape of Beethoven's Ninth. When he comes we will hike together. Up and down Murphy's Hill. God's leftovers. And if someone asks my Sherpa friend, "How far did you walk today?" he'll look at me and I'll look at him. And we'll smile.

19. The Tag Sale

———❧———

Value lies in the eyes of the beholder.

I was three years old when big and furry Purple Panda entered my life to live with me for fifty years. The stuffed Purple Panda swelled with pride when I graduated from Brown University, spent a year abroad in Israel, and learned Hebrew at the seminary. Yes, Panda and I were inseparable. Despite the loss of a plastic eye and a leg ripped off sometime in the World War II period, Panda survived. Until Marion. Marion was not a saver. For fifteen years Purple Panda barely escaped the rubbish heap. While the children were young, Panda stayed with them; but when Chris refused to welcome Panda in his Wall Street office (despite a bear market), I knew Panda's days were numbered.

One morning Marion gathered Panda, my 1945 Kodak with

the missing shutter, a blowgun from the Amazon Indians (acquired in a trade for two dead Eveready flashlight batteries), four automobile tires of assorted sizes, and rusty fishing lures. The time had come, Marion explained, to dispose of these treasures of the past. I sank into depression, and even the lovely poem of Emma Lazarus failed to raise my spirit: "Give me your tires, your lures, / The wretched refuse of your teeming floors, etc., etc."

Then in the wee hours of night I heard a voice, a soothing voice. "Dan, Dan." Who was speaking? "Dan, Dan. Come here. Over to the window. Look out on your rhubarb field. Look. Look." So I looked out at the acres and acres of rhubarb field behind my field, and in the field were families dressed in old clothes playing tag. And the voice returned. "If you sell it they will come. If you sell it they will come." And I knew what I must do with Panda, the shutterless Kodak, and the Valentine card from Grace, my sixth-grade sweetheart. I must have a tag sale. "If you sell it they will come."

That is how we decided to have a tag sale on a bright spring day in early June. Goods, the finest goods, sprawled over the lawn. One-of-a-kind items. One gold earring. One chip in the plastic ashtray. One rip in the faded lampshade. And one Panda. Jaguars, Mercedes, BMWs climbed Murphy's Hill, drawn by the promise of free lemonade, free coffee, and the rare opportunity to buy my lifetime. I even threw in the straw hat with a red band and the number '55, presented to me at my twentieth high school class reunion. By 10:30 A.M. several dozen amateur and professional antique dealers had studied my exquisite possessions. I wandered over to Marion behind the cash register. "Well, how am I doing?"

"Not too well," Marion answered. "In fact, not a sale. I would also suggest reducing Panda's price. Someone picked him up by the ears and the head fell off."

At that moment a brawny man dressed in khaki fatigues

and carrying a deer-hunting gun sauntered over to the cash register. "Any sets of toy soldiers? I'm looking for British artillery men from World War II."

I led him over to the Amazon Indian blowgun and explained: "When they stormed the beaches at Normandy, the Allied forces were led by a crack tribe of Amazon Indians, and it just so happens that I have one of the blowguns used by those Indians at Normandy. Good price. What do you say?" The hunter said I didn't know very much about Normandy, but he had a book about World War II in his car and he would sell me the book for $24.95. Our tag sale was now $24.95 in debt.

Misfortune increased when someone stole the empty cash register during Marion's lunch break. Then at 2:30 P.M., he came. The man in the Volkswagen van. The van could hold our entire tag sale and the Van Man offered to negotiate. We entered into intense discussion as Marion munched popcorn and watched from the distance. At 3:30 P.M. close to agreement. At 4:00 P.M. the deal was sealed! I shouted over to Marion, "Break out the lemonade, we've got a deal!" The Van Man and I shook hands and I reached into my wallet and took out a ten-dollar bill. After I handed him the money, he reached down, picked up Panda, body and head, and disappeared into his car. I gave Marion a bear hug. "Success! We got rid of Panda and it only cost us ten dollars."

By dusk we had returned the Kodak, fishing lures, straw hat, blowgun, and tires to their home in the attic. Reflecting on the day's activities, I concluded that one person's past is not necessarily another person's future. In fact, each one of us has his own storehouse of wonders. Objects, events, people, important to me. Maybe not to you. But never mind. Value lies in the eye of the beholder.

20. The Quiet Hour

———⟳———

The quiet hour, 11:00 P.M. The snuggling hour. Deep, deep under the feather quilt. Just me. And Marion. And a book of 975 pages. I'm lost in the jungles of Ecuador. Or traveling the Orient Express. Hiking in Provence. Absorbed in a biography of Michelangelo, JFK. The quiet hour when the world is silent and only the written word can be heard in the solitude of the mind. Outside, dogwood branches gently rub against the windowpane and a wind chime caresses the air with a nighttime melody. The quiet hour.

But hark! A sound cometh from the far side of the bed where my spouse lieth. Many sounds. And what are these strange sounds reverberating through the quiet hour? Marion crunching popcorn. Marion listening to the 11:00 P.M. news on television. Marion playing the sound track from *Les Misérables* on a tape recorder. Marion crinkling the *New York Times.* Turning pages. During the quiet hour. The sacred hour before night spreads her pinion of sleep over the universe. (Whatever that means!)

"Ears, Marion! Ears!" I am incensed, and the news report shifts to Geraldo on domestic violence as my warning cry storms the barricades of *Les Misérables.* The *Times* withers and the popcorn pops out of the bowl. "Ears, Marion! Ears." This is a signal for Marion to put on earphones and shove the popcorn under the bed. I want quiet in the quiet hour.

Noise. I was born in the age of noise. Marion cannot fall asleep to the sound of quiet. Scott cannot study unless the TV is turned to full volume. Chris washes his car with every tweet of the tweeter tweeting and every woof of the woofer woofing. Even the summer's thunderstorms are louder. No wonder. How else can God be heard? I ask you, "When did the Grinch steal quiet?" Speak up.

Once it was different. When I was a youngster I lived in a quiet home. I was a first-born child. A last-born child. An only child. We were a nuclear family. Before the explosion. After dinner Dad would uncover his orange pen and write sermons. My mother, a social worker, would settle into the old chair and read *The Life of Freud.* Freud lived a long time. Mom was on volume four. I was left to rummage with our dog, Hoppy, a Boston terrier who, in fifteen years of a dog's life, only barked twice. By accident. We were a family at home with silence.

And now! Noise! Noise! Noise! Even in the country, far removed from police sirens and fire engines. Noise! From Marion my beloved spouse. "Ears, Marion! Ears!" How many years have I yelled "Ears"? But recently Marion has changed. I date her transformation to an experience this past summer when we visited St. Martin's of Canigou, a Benedictine abbey in the French Pyrenees. Since the eleventh century, Benedictine monks have lived in the abbey, a craggy monastery blending into a rock cliff. Before we entered the cloister, cut off from the outside world, a nun explained the history of the abbey. Construction beginning in the year 1000; the tombs of Count Guilfred and his second wife, Countess Elizabeth, who retired to the abbey in 1035; the earthquake of 1428. A video followed the nun's presentation and explained the stone capitals decorating the cloister—lions, stylized leaves, gospel stories.

When the video concluded, the nun entertained questions.

"Yes, the monastery was deserted from 1782 until 1982."

"Yes, the monastery is served from the town of Perpignan."

Then Marion asked a question. "Excuse me, in what language will the tour be given? Spanish? French? Maybe English?"

The nun smiled and straightened her beige robe. "In the Abbey of St. Martin of Canigou we have taken a vow of silence. No one speaks. The tour will be in the language of silence."

The language of silence. We were entering a place where no one spoke. Marion turned white. I knew what she was thinking. Who would want to live in silence? Listen to themselves? No place to run from the inner voice. Wow! Scary! Come on. St. Martin's, keep in step with the times. Bang the gongs. Ring the bells. Send the chants tumbling down the mountainside. I'll send you my *Les Miz* tape, a VCR of Geraldo. We have an extra popcorn maker. Two popcorn makers. Three. Four. A popcorn maker with a built-in generator. In case of a power failure. They're yours, St. Martin's. Even my king-size bed. How many abbeys have a king-size bed? A mix of church and state. But I won't send you Marion. Not a chance. The experience at St. Martin's dulled her love of noise. She's good now. Very good. And I don't even say, "Ears, Marion! Ears."

At the quiet hour we say in a soft voice, "The language of silence."

Then we settle back and listen to the dogwood, the wind chime, and ourselves.

Sshh! It's the quiet hour.

Good night.

21. Gutter Day

～◎～

On the last day of spring cleanup, Tripp Street celebrates Gutter Day. The day begins with a parade of Tripp Streeters carrying ladders, and I can assure you the scene is mighty impressive. Max, ramrod straight, carrying his sixteen-footer. Old Luke in torn flannel pants, scuffed work boots, and a ladder missing two rungs. Garth carries a spiffy chartreuse stepladder from Leonard's Ladder Boutique. In front of the reviewing stand (wooden bleachers on Mrs. Martha Parsons's lawn) Otto pulls on the string of his extension ladder and the top eight feet pop up in a snappy salute. Mrs. Martha Parsons anoints each ladder with a handful of leaves and calls out, "Hear ye, hear ye, ladders to the gutters." Gutter Day has officially begun.

Soon a battalion of ladders line the homes on Tripp Street and residents scamper up to clean leaves out of the gutters and free the roof drains. I am not part of the neighborhood effort. On Gutter Day I make an appropriate excuse and disappear. "What? This Saturday is Gutter Day? Oh, I'm sorry but I can't be here. We have our Sabbath services."

"Don't worry," Otto responds. "We'll be at it all afternoon. You can join us later in the day."

I smile at Otto. "Sure would like to, but I don't know whether I can be home in time. But while you're up on the roof, just think of me praying. Who knows, I may be even higher."

After several years of excuses no one bothers to invite me to Gutter Day. Fortunately I am still included in Rake Day and Cucumber Day celebrations and never miss a meeting of the Tripp Street Pothole Association, but I detour from Gutter Day. The explanation is really quite simple. I'm afraid of heights. Even when I was a child and the Mallery Place Gang in Wilkes-Barre slept out in their tree house, I set up my pup tent and slept at the foot of the tree. Although I can scamper up a ladder with the best of them, I can't come down. I create vertical traffic jams. A psychologist once suggested that choosing the rabbinate may have been predicated on my fear of heights. "Unable to surmount your fear of physical heights, you have chosen to concentrate on spiritual heights." Someday I will seek a second opinion.

But last year, to the astonishment of my neighbors, I appeared on Gutter Day with ladder in hand—a special ladder with infinite extensions. A bonus for laboring in the Fields of the Lord. Or as they said at seminary: A Hot Line to God. Yes, I appeared on Gutter Day, but I did not intend to ascend to my rooftop. No, I had a stand-in. Chris. My rock-climbing son who recently accomplished the difficult task of scaling our stone chimney. Chris would clean the gutter. And before I knew it, he was squishing around in the wet leaves lining my roof.

Then a strange thing happened. Chris invited me to join him on the roof, and in spite of my vow to always stay on firm ground, I climbed up and teetered and tottered on the edge of the roof. Why did I listen to my son? Was I responding to the prophetic words "And a young child shall lead them"? But that wasn't even my religion. Who can explain why, after careful thought and planning, we occasionally act on a whim?

Gradually I acclimated and ventured over to the chimney peak, where Chris pointed to the east. Over Crooks Notch I could see sailboats on Long Island Sound. My eye traveled across the Atlantic. "Chris, look, there's the QE2 and Europe." I could barely make out Pierre and Françoise drinking café on the Left Bank and Hans bringing his cows in from a pasture nestled in the Swiss Alps. Chris had focused on the French Riviera, where a blond woman covered only by a pearl necklace and earring bronzed on golden sand. "Just like summers at Heron Pond. Right, Chris?" He blushed and we shared one of those intimate moments enjoyed by a father and son perched on the rooftop on Gutter Day.

At 5:00 P.M. Old Luke released thirty helium balloons emblazoned with the words "Gutter Day" and we reassembled on Mrs. Parsons's lawn for closing ceremonies. Dumping our bags of leaves in Mrs. Parsons's garden, where they would rot until Mulch Day in May, we circled the pile seven times, and then a hush fell over the street. "This year the closing address will be given by Dan," Mrs. Martha Parsons announced. "In honor of the height he has reached in his own life." Pride soared in my heart as I unrolled the parchment scroll and launched into my speech, "What Gutter Day Means to Me, by Dan No Longer Afraid of Heights." A murmur of approval spread through the crowd.

"Gutter Day means to me the need to take risks in life. To leave the ground, rise above our fears, and look to distant horizons; to see gutters on Tripp Street, cafés in Paris, cows in Switzerland. That's what Gutter Day means to me."

A mighty roar reverberated along Tripp Street as I climbed down from the podium and headed off in search of new heights to scale.

22. Buying Eyeglasses

I am aging. I never knew it until the day I went to Homer's Opticians for new glasses and returned home with a pair of brown frames. Marchon #53017, made in Italy. The frames, unoccupied by lenses, stare at me from a lucite stand mounted on my desk. Who would buy a pair of eyeglasses without lenses? Me. Why? To remind me that I am aging. Moving from decade to decade.

The rite of passage began innocently enough with a visit to Homer's. When Homer saw me enter he smiled. "Dan, I haven't seen you in years. How are you?"

"Hasn't been a good year, Homer. The dentist found five cavities only a month after he assured me my teeth had run out of room for fillings. I had always believed that 'he who maximizes decay at an early age discovers little room for ruin in later years.' I was wrong and I've been in and out of the dentist. Now I also need bifocals."

"Well, Dan, let's see what we can do. First, pick out some frames."

I protested. "Homer, I intend to use my old frames. The ones I'm wearing."

Homer grimaced. "Dan, those pink tortoiseshells are out of fashion. Anyway, they look in pretty bad shape."

"Bad shape?"

"Definitely. The screws are missing."

"No problem, Homer. I fixed them with Krazy Glue."

"And the crack in the left side?"

"Cape Cod. The summer of seventy-two. They fell on a rock. But the right side's fine except for the mold near the rim."

"Dan, I appreciate your loyalty to the frames, but I can't do anything with them."

That's when I entered the modern world of haute couture eyeglasses. Vuarnet for the French look. Serengeti Eyewear for the armchair reader embarked on fantasies of hunting lions in East Africa. Porsche Design by Carrera, guaranteed to increase your reading speed from twenty words per minute to ninety. Yes, as the poster boasted, I had walked into "A Rainbow of Fashion. If a Face Is Like a Work of Art, It Deserves a Good Frame." My face a work of art? A smattering of freckles, a collage of wrinkles, a dab of dimple? A Leonardo masterpiece or a common reproduction? How could I decide which glasses to buy in this post-tortoiseshell era? On appearance? On health considerations? Certain frames were advertised as "lighter and thinner." Would they cut down my cholesterol? Instead of the enlightenment offered by a new prescription, my visit to Homer's Opticians had clouded my vision.

The time passed. Customers came and went. Homer reminded me, "Dan, we close at five." At 4:55 I made the decision. Thin brown Italian frames Marchon #53017. Proudly I strode up to Homer, who was polishing a pair of aviator glasses.

"Here, Homer."

Homer took the brown frames. "Good choice, Dan. But why did you choose these frames?"

I thought for a moment. "I decided to make a fashion statement. Isn't that what you're supposed to do?"

Homer nodded. "But why this pair? Why brown?"

"Well, Homer, I decided to purchase frames that would match my hair. Color coordinate and all that."

Homer looked at me. Then at my hair. Then he giggled and called to his assistant, Vivian, who was grinding lenses.

"Vivian, Dan bought these brown frames to match his hair." Then Vivian giggled. Then Homer and Vivian giggled. Then I blushed.

Homer held up a mirror. "Take a look at yourself, Dan." I looked. My hair was silver. An occasional strand of brown gasped for breathing room, but my hair was silver. When had this color change occurred? In the last hour? Shopping for glasses? Of course not.

Why had I forgotten the gradual passage of time, from brown to gray? The children had grown, my mother had died, and my hair had turned silver. The world around me had definitely grown older. Why didn't I acknowledge the change? Why did I still feel brown? Thank God I did! Let outside events mark the inevitable passage of events. Outside events. But what will happen on my next visit to Homer? Will I be bald? Will I need frameless frames?

The clock struck five, and Homer waited for my decision. "Do you want the brown frames?"

"Yes. But I also want a pair of silver frames." Then I whispered, "Put the new prescription in the silver frames and leave the brown ones empty."

I left Homer's Opticians with the two frames. I wear the

silver glasses, and the brown frames remain on my desk, resting on a Lucite stand. Occasionally I set the silver frames next to their brown relatives. Together they help me see where I was and where I am. Subtle reminders of the flow of time.

23. Nails in an Ashtray

⟨⟩

The past lies in an ashtray on my desk; rusty square nails with the musty smell of age. The nails came out of our Yankee gutters, part of the house since 1861. Mike the Carpenter brought the sad news of the gutters when he climbed onto the roof and returned with a handful of rotten wood pulp.

"Got to do something about these gutters," he warned. "Amazed they lasted this long. Almost a hundred fifty years. That's a hundred forty-seven years longer than my toaster oven lasted. My suggestion is to put up aluminum gutters."

But Marion and I wanted to restore the old Yankee gutters—wooden beams with a hand-milled trough for drainage.

"Mike, you think you can do Yankee gutters?"

"Tell you the truth, Dan, never seen one in the old country, but a gutter's a gutter—even a Yankee gutter." So Mike

Spazzioli tore down the rotten Yankee gutter and took measurements for the renovation.

"Back to you as soon as I find the wood. Seventy feet of four-by-ten-inch wood. When I'm done it'll be good as new." I hoped he meant good as old.

A week passed. Two weeks. A month. Mike called. "Got a problem. No one makes four-by-ten Yankee gutters anymore. I can get you a four-by-six but not a four-by-ten. Any ideas?"

"Keep looking, Mike. I'll make some calls too." I tried Bloomingdale's, Land's End, Victoria's Secret, and Rosebud Nursery. Rosebud came closest. "Mister, for $39.50 I'll sell you a four-foot hickory tree. Should produce four-by-ten-inch logs in ten or fifteen years. How many you want?" That's what Rosebud said.

I advertised in the *New York Times Magazine* section next to ads for $1,200,000 houses on Oyster Bay and Snoots Landing. "Wanted, all the gutter that's fit to utter. Call 914-666-6666." Bubbles, Marion's friend from Palm Beach, called to tell us she thought the ad was "sooo cute," and we simply had to have a party featuring a gutter motif. No one answered the ad.

More time passed. March winds infiltrated the roof through the open spaces where not too long ago we at least had a rotten Yankee gutter. Mike! Mike! Why did you destroy the old gutter before you had a replacement? That weekend at services I gave a sermon entitled "Do Not Tear Down Unless You Are Able to Rebuild." I received many compliments on this sermon, even from Arthur, my constant critic. "Dan, this time you really spoke from the heart."

"No, Arthur, this time I really spoke from the roof."

It was Scott who resolved our dilemma. Home from college, he disappeared into the den and went to work on his computers and calculators. When Scott finally resurfaced, he called, "Dan, Mike, Teddy!" (We included Teddy in carpentry discussions because, as a retriever of sticks and a chewer of chair legs, she was into wood.) Scott passed out pencil and paper.

"After creating a sophisticated computer program I have a solution. We can find a four-by-six-inch Yankee gutter but not a four-by-ten. Right?" Mike and I nodded. Teddy chewed on her pencil and barked. "Well, if we put a four-by-four behind the four-by-six we'll have a four-by-ten. Understand?" I didn't understand a word of Scott's higher math, but Mike embraced him, called my son a genius, and rushed out to the lumber yard.

The next day he was banging away on the roof as I watched from down below. "Mike, it doesn't look right. Having two pieces of wood instead of one."

Mike scoffed. "What did you expect. You know you can't replace the past!"

He was right. Not even with a computer or with a four-by-six plus a four-by-four that equals four-by-ten. That night I went to the rubbish pile and patted the remains of the original Yankee gutters. I even offered a final benediction, a variation on "dust to dust, ashes to ashes." "Splinters to splinters, wood chips to wood chips." Then I pulled out the rusty square nails and placed them in the ashtray on my desk.

Time moves on relentlessly. The past slides by, never to reappear. Only the nails remain.

24. The Asplundh Man

———◉———

Every spring the Asplundh man visits Tripp Street bringing loss in his wake. You can hear the wheels of his truck crunching gravel as he maneuvers the narrow turn beyond Otto's house. Last year he took a section of stone wall, but the Asplundh man can't be bothered with earthly concerns. Master tree pruner, the Asplundh man lives above this world, cutting off branches that grew on Tripp Street long before he rose to the heavens in an orange cherry picker.

When I first heard the limbs crashing to the ground I grimaced and promised my trees, "Don't worry, he'll never come here. Not on our property." But times change, and a year came when the maple shading our house threatened the roof. It was Foster who sounded the alarm. "Dan, you'd better call the Asplundh man. Your maple's top-heavy."

I protested. "Not on your life, Foster."

Foster shrugged. "I don't care. It's not my house."

I knew Foster was right, so one morning at six I drove into town to find the Asplundh man. He always sat in his truck at that hour, wiry limbs draped over the steering wheel, drinking a cup of coffee in front of Bob's Stationery Store.

"Morning," I called to the Asplundh man.

"Morning," he answered.

I hesitated.

"Well?" he asked.

"I have a maple tree leaning against my house. Want a job when you're off work?"

A malevolent smile spread across the face of the Asplundh man. Two gold teeth framed a cavernous space in his mouth. He rubbed his hands together in delight. "Sure thing. I'll be over tonight to give an estimate."

Maybe he wouldn't come. Maybe my tree would be saved. Not a chance. The Asplundh man smelled sap, and at 7:00 P.M. the doorbell rang.

"Looked at your maple," he said. "Needs an amputation on the right side."

My wife turned white. I hadn't seen her like this since her fingernail split.

"We'll think about it," I answered.

That night our family convened in conference. Our son the economist approved the Big Cut. "We can sell the logs for firewood."

Our son the doctor suggested a second opinion. "He's not the only tree pruner in town."

My wife disappeared into a bowl of popcorn.

But we knew. We didn't have a choice. I was elected to deal with the Asplundh man. A second 6:00 A.M. confrontation in front of Bob's.

"What do you say we compromise? Take a few branches off now, a few more next month," I suggested.

The Asplundh man scoffed. "What's the big deal? It's only a tree. A hundred years or so and you'll never know it happened. Limbs grow back." The Asplundh man had more faith in eternity than I'll ever have.

He did it. Late one afternoon. I pulled into the driveway just in time to watch him wipe the last drops of sap off his saw. Our neighbor's dog, Wallace, a blind cocker spaniel, paced the yard looking for a place to lift his leg. The Asplundh man had removed Wallace's favorite watering spot. And that night I couldn't sleep. I tossed. I turned. I had a nightmare. In the dream I rocked in the old wicker chair on the front porch. Suddenly three wooden branches appeared near the purple wisteria. One branch, gnarled and bowed under the weight of time, dropped a brown leaf in my lap; the second branch, lithe and graceful, shimmied under her veil of green leaves; and the third branch, scarcely more than a shoot, hung on to the bark of the other two. Then, before my eyes, the petals of the wisteria turned into metal teeth attacking the three branches. Soon only a pile of sawdust remained on my porch.

When morning came, mourning came. I looked out the window. Where once a giant limb had shaded the bedroom, there was open space. Would I ever adjust to the missing limbs? Worse still, would Wallace ever go to the bathroom again? Of course our sons remained unmoved by the experience. Scott the almost doctor praised the Asplundh man's surgical skill. Chris the economist calculated that the ground wood pulp would produce sufficient paper for one hundred *Wall Street Journals*.

Foster stopped by. "So you did it. Makes sense. Makes a lot of sense." Foster looks at life philosophically. He always has. "Life is an unending cycle of limbing and de-limbing." Good old Foster; always around for a word of comfort.

The seasons changed. Spring blossomed into summer. And I changed. Slowly. Maybe it was the course I taught on "Death and Dying" at the high schools. "Now, students, we can surmount loss. Trust time and the regenerative powers." I had some doubt about my words, but eventually I did forget the Big Cut. Sure, I missed the old limbs, but the scar had turned a dull gray, the tufted titmouse played on the trunk, Wallace again lifted his leg. And someday baby shoots would emerge from the trunk near the missing branches. So I reason that if a tree can dig down to its roots and start over, why can't I? Find new beginnings beneath the earth or within the self—that's what life is all about.

Not too long ago the doorbell rang. An orange truck hovered in the driveway and the Asplundh man waved his hand in greeting. "Mind if I stop by with the Varicks later today? They live up on Barnes Lane and need some trees cut. I gave your name as a reference. Told them you were one of my better jobs."

And I was. In the world of the Asplundh man. One of his better jobs? Well, I guess I was.

25. The Cracks Between the Floorboards

~~~

In the beginning God created the heavens, the earth, and the floorboards. So who created the cracks between the floorboards? In 1861, when my house was under construction, someone dropped an armful of cracks between the twelve-inch pine floorboards. From my bedroom I can look down into the living room, and from the living room into the basement. Since I first moved into the house I have searched for the answer to my dilemma. Who created the space between the floorboards? No one knows. Not even the town historian. This particular architectural knowledge has fallen between the cracks.

Who cares? you ask. But consider well. Everything in life has a purpose. Even life's gaps. Unfortunately we live in a time when insufficient attention is paid to empty space. Floorboards are only one example. Consider doughnuts. Do doughnut lovers ever speak of the hole in the middle of the doughnut? Of course not. The hole is nothing more than wasted space. Occasionally children acknowledge a doughnut hole by inserting a finger into the hole and twirling the doughnut, but that is only an afterthought. Life Savers. The same problem. Once we suck a peppermint Life Saver down to the hole we think we are finished. Nonsense! Savor that hole!

Back to the cracks in the floorboards. My lawyer friend Henry wants to fill in the cracks. The other evening he stopped by with a tube of Elmer's Caulking Paste sticking out of the watch pocket of his pinstripe vest. How many lawyers squeeze into the 6:09 from Grand Central Station with a tube of caulking paste stuck into their suit? But Henry was on a mission. "Dan, whenever I sit on your kitchen stool I see the light from the basement shining up through the cracks. That shouldn't be. Space was created to be filled." And with that, Hank pulled out his Elmer's Caulking Paste. Unfortunately the tube had leaked somewhere between Scarsdale and North White Plains, filling the buttonholes of his vest and fastening the vest to his body. After cutting him out of the vest, I suggested we discuss the issue.

"Hank, why do you look down upon cracks?"

Hank, always a stickler for language, replied, "I do not look down upon cracks. I look down between cracks."

Never argue with lawyers.

"Hank, you know what I mean. You assume the cracks shouldn't be there. I'm not so sure. There is a theory that first God created cracks. Huge cracks. Then God filled in the space with floorboards, but no one was happy. The boards wanted space. The cracks wanted space. So the boards shrank from one another and the cracks expanded. Everyone was happier with room to breathe and spread out. Now you come along and want to reverse the order. Do you understand?"

Of course Henry didn't understand. How could he? Fresh from a day in New York, where he had negotiated a contract to build a shopping center on an empty field along Palisades Parkway. But I continued. "Hank, I love to see the basement light shimmer between the cracks. When the light sneaks up I gain insight. My kitchen has a hundred doors."

Hank fidgeted on the kitchen stool and grabbed on to Elmer's for security.

"What about rock climbers, Hank?"

"What about them?"

"How do you think they challenge a sheer cliff? Beyond ropes and pins they search for cracks, crevices in the cliff where they find a grip, then pull themselves up. They use those crevices to ascend to the next level. Without those empty spaces to hold on to, to pause and look down on where they've been, they can't go higher."

Hank forced a glob of caulk into a paper cup. Then he asked, "What about everything you lose in the cracks? Food falling off the table."

I laughed. "Food? With Teddy of Hopeless Junction standing by? Not a chance. It's not what I lose in the cracks. It's what I find. Yesterday Marion and I stretched out on the floor and discovered two straight pins and a quarter. Last week we found a pearl, probably dropped years ago. Henry, I know this is hard for you to understand, but what you might see as cracks or emptiness or barren land I see as a spawning ground for treasures. Look between the floorboards. Run over a meadow still unspoiled by buildings or by progress. Savor the fullness. Of emptiness. Think about it, Henry. Think about it."

But when I looked up I realized I had been talking to empty space. Henry had slipped out through a crack in the front door.

26. Scott

"**D**ad, if you had been born a hundred and fifty years ago, the Industrial Revolution never would have happened!"

I beamed. "Thanks for the compliment, son."

Scott grimaced and went back to his computer. You see, Scott and I represent different generations. He is a child of the technological age. And I? A remnant of the past; mired in the time of Tyrannosaurus Rex. Dinosaurs. Big Red Pens. That's what really gets to Scott. Big Red Pens. Whenever Scott sees me slumped over a yellow pad writing in longhand, refilling Big Red in an inkwell, he lets out an embarrassed laugh.

"Dad, you're old-fashioned; out of touch with the times."

I protested. "How can you say that? We're the only family on the block with a Teenage Mutant Ninja Turtle!"

Scott was not amused. Instead, sparks of missionary zeal

shot from his blue eyes. "That's not what I mean, Dad. You need a word processor, a VCR, a fax."

The sounds "word processor," "VCR," "fax" roll out of Scott like the words "divine," "heaven," "The Holy One, blessed be He" flow from my mouth when I give a weekly sermon. And speaking of "The Holy One," did God use a computer when He created the world? And, over seven days, was His system ever down? Of course not! Sure, God made a few mistakes, like snakes and broccoli, but even if He had caught these infractions on instant replay, would it have made a difference? So why do I need a computer for my earthly concerns? Call me Tyrannosaurus Rex if you want. Erase me from your memory bank. I don't care. I would rather be a Rex than a Fax.

I confess, computers never turned me on. My friends in the city listen for a call-waiting click; at my home in the country I study what makes a deer tick. What's the hurry? On Tripp Street we still live in the era B.C. Before Computers.

Or used to. Now I detect signs of change. Everywhere. Even in my rural hamlet. For instance, the local truck stop recently hung a computer-designed pink sign in the window. "Come in and See Our New Arrival!" At first I thought Kelly had had her baby. About time! She could hardly reach over the counter to hand me a cup of coffee. Decaf. But then I saw Kelly dishing out chopped chicken liver and still pregnant. Very. So I re-read the sign. "Come In and See Our New Arrival! Kelly's Truck Stop Proudly Announces the Arrival of a New Fax Machine. Fax in Your Orders—666-5734." And sure enough, there was Sophie Flater, the hairdresser at Off the Top, faxing in an urgent order for one poppyseed bagel. Sergeant McElroy faxed in his usual cream cheese and mustard on pumpernickel. I seemed to be the only one ordering in person and, slightly self-conscious, whispered, "Lean corn beef on rye." Kelly gave me one of those patronizing smiles that suggested "How quaint!"

Our town is fax infested, from Pete's Pizza to Guy's Gulf Station. And how long can I hold out? When will I become a mere dot on the matrix of life? Scott knows. Time is on his side. Someday yellow pads, already an endangered species, will enter the annals of history. (The local stationery store offers yellow pads at 40 percent off. The next step? Final Clearance. And then? Extinction. Soon, too soon, I will be called upon to offer memorial prayers for the yellow pad, erased from earthly existence.) Will I be next? Wiped off life's screen? No! Never! I am changing, slowly succumbing to the web of high technology. Ah, how are the mighty fallen!

Yesterday, while Scott checked airline schedules on his computer, he caught me lurking in the hall.

"Come on in," he called.

I hesitated.

"Dad, what do you think? I have to fly to Chicago for the med school interview. Should I take United's Flight 846? Breakfast features croissants, raspberry jam, bacon and eggs; in-flight movie *Rocky I*. Sounds good. But if I take Northwest they're showing *M*A*S*H*.*"

"All that's on the computer?" I asked.

"Sure. The entire scene at 33,000 feet. And higher."

"And higher." Looking back, I believe those two words shook my faith in the eternal verities. Knocked the bottom out of my pile of yellow pads. Tore me apart. Burst my printout. Those two words "And higher." Why? Well, if Scott could plot the terrain at 33,000 feet, almost the foothills of heaven, could I make contact with God hovering a byte higher? I know! I know! Ridiculous. I must be running a fever. Hallucinating. The flu? Pneumonia? Computer virus? Or do my symptoms indicate an advanced state of desperation? Will I pursue any possibility of a one-on-one encounter with God? That's it! A one-on-one encounter. Face to face. Or fax to fax. After all, last week I dialed 1-800-GOD-HEAR on the toy phone left at my pulpit after the Sunday School play. God did not hear. Fortunately, neither did any of my congregants.

But I am ripe for technology theology, and Scott thinks he can program me away from yellow pads and Big Red. So this afternoon he entered my study for a serious conversation.

"Dad?"

"Yes, son."

"We need to have a little talk."

Scott blushed and I succumbed to a moment of nostalgia. It seemed only yesterday that my son had sat on my laptop. And now? A real son-to-dad talk.

"It's okay, son. I'm your dad. You can tell me anything. Still having trouble with Daisy what's-her-name? Daisy Printer. Too bad. You seemed to like her."

Scott, always the literalist, corrected my gaff. "Dad, the term is daisy wheel printer and, no, that's not the problem. Sit down." With that he pulled out a tattered copy of the *Revised Standard Version User's Manual* and in a serious voice, punctuated with a series of beeps, Scott read: "In the beginning God created the heaven and the earth, and all that was therein. And He worked. And He worked. And on the seventh day He placed the world on cruise control and He rested."

And that is how Scott began the subtle conversion of my house to the brave new world of technology.

Summer

27. Weed Day

Weed Day. Those of us living on Tripp Street celebrate Weed Day on the day after the bittersweet on my property strangles the sweet peas growing on Garth's fence. This usually coincides with the day when Old Luke's thistles measure in at ten inches, or the first week in June. According to Tripp Street history, Weed Day was originally called Common Weed Day, but "Common" was dropped in 1971 to improve our image. There is nothing common about Tripp Street, not even the weeds. They grow into the heavens, and in sheer number they are more numerous than the stars. We are the weed center of the world!

As with all major holidays, Weed Day begins on Mrs. Martha Parsons's lawn, and in honor of this particular day we recite Royce Filmer's beautiful poem "Weeds."

I think that I will always seed
My garden with the common weed,
A weed that mocks my work all day
And sprouts as if it's A-O.K.,
A weed that may in summer wear
A slug or snail that's on the tear,
A weed whose ugly root is pressed
Beneath the earth when I am stressed.
Upon whose bosom my hoe has lain,
Who comes right back with cold disdain.
Weeds are sown by fools like me,
And God looks down and says tee-hee.

(With grateful acknowledgment to Rose, Ruth, Sadie, and Gerty, who still remember the original words.)

At the words "tee-hee," Old Luke, Max, Otto, Leatrice, Garth, Hank, and I return to our gardens and begin the chore of weeding. Up down. Up down. Occasionally we break for a cup of dandelion juice tinged with wild onion and a sprig of crabgrass floating on the top. So the time passes. Weed Day on Tripp Street.

But this year I protested and failed to appear for the ritual reading of "I think that I will always seed." I would celebrate Weed Day in my own fashion. With Tom. Tom from the nursery, who backed into my driveway with a dump truck filled with five yards of pine shavings and mulch. I had called Tom several days before, when the bittersweet tentacles tentatively touched the sweet pea and I knew Weed Day was fast approaching.

"Tom," I said, "I need five yards of pine shaving mulch. Instead of weeding, I'm mulching."

At the other end of the phone Tom asked, "How many men should I send to shovel the mulch?"

Supremely confident, I replied, "None. I'll do it myself."

Tom laughed. "Do you know how much five yards of mulch is?"

I stared at a yardstick hanging on the other side of the kitchen. It didn't look very long to me.

On Weed Day Tom pulled in and parked under a huge banner draped across the driveway: "If You Can't Weed 'em Mulch 'em!" Hanging from the sign were three bunches of ragweed swinging in effigy.

Tom opened the back of the dump truck and the shavings came tumbling out, much to the discomfort of Teddy, who, doing her morning business, was almost mulched. I soothed the dog. "No, Teddy, a mutt is not a weed." Then I looked at my driveway. A brown mountain covered the entranceway. After cursing the yardstick for fraudulent advertising, I started shoveling. Where the weeds were deepest I applied more mulch. By midday, mounds of shavings covered the poison ivy, bittersweet, and thistles. From dawn to dusk I labored in the Fields of the Lord. In the distance I heard my neighbors reassemble at Mrs. Martha Parsons's for Weed Day closing ceremonies and the final benediction.

> *I know that I will never need*
> *To have my garden fill with weed.*
> *If I just bend and work all day,*
> *At dusk I'll have the final say.*

Not me. I labored in the Fields of the Lord for four days before the weeds were mulched. As it says in our liturgy, "Day followed day in endless succession," and Advil followed Motrin, and Ben-Gay followed Advil. Also in endless succession. Finally I stepped back. My yard was a beautiful sea of brown pine shavings. Otto, Max, and Jason stopped by to congratulate me on my creativity, but Old Luke just shook his head. "It'll never work, Dan. Never work."

"Skeptic!" I shouted. "Ye of little faith!"

But Old Luke was right. Within a week I learned the bittersweet truth about mulching. The bittersweet was back. And the poison ivy and the thistles. Stronger than ever. Old Luke came by. To gloat? Not on Tripp Street. To comfort. "Like everything else in life," he said in his soft Yankee drawl, "can't get rid of your problems by covering them over. Got to get rid of them. You should've pulled the weeds out. Yep, weed first, mulch later. If it weren't true we wouldn't be celebrating Weed Day for forty-nine years. Wouldn't be a fixture on the Tripp Street calendar."

I assured Luke when Weed Day rolled around again I would be there, at Mrs. Martha Parsons's and my voice would lead the Poets' Corner

> *I think that I will always seed*
> *My garden with the common weed,*
> *A weed that pushes through its cover,*
> *Embarrassing even the mulch lover.*
> *For weeds, though sown by fools like me,*
> *Are best pulled out while on one knee.*

28. Some Assembly Required

~~~~~~◎~~~~~~

At 4:15 P.M., on his way to apprehend a killer rabbit OD-ing on Otto's carrot patch, Police Officer Kevin Kelly put out an all-points bulletin in the case of the missing hole. My missing hole. Officer Kelly successfully arrested the rabbit but reported failure in the case of the missing hole. I was hysterical. This was not just any hole. This hole was crucial for attaching the left leg to the seat of my build-it-yourself Adirondack Chair Kit.

It had all looked so easy when I stopped at Floyd's Lumber to purchase Adirondack chairs for my lawn.

> *One little, two little, three little Adirondack,*
> *Four little, five little, six little Adirondack,*

Seven little, eight little, nine little Adirondack,
Ten little Adirondack chairs

sat in front of the store.

A sign announced "Special Sale $49.95." In the far chair a burly salesman slumped in slumber, the brim of a Mike's Mechanics cap covering his eyes. Did I have the heart to wake him or should I turn out the fluorescent lights and let Mike sleep? I could always return later. But how would I know when he was awake? Feeling guilty, I nudged Mike. He opened his right eye. "Sorry to disturb you, sir, but could you tell me your waking hours? I want to buy some Adirondack chairs."

"Buddy, I'm awake every afternoon between three-fifteen and three-twenty-five, but I'll make an exception for you." Then he closed his eyes and went back to sleep. Another shake. He mumbled, "Leave the check on the counter."

"But, sir," I countered, "you're sleeping in one of the chairs I want." This time Mike opened his left eye. At least I was dealing with an ambidextrous salesman.

"These chairs aren't for sale," he said in a barely audible voice. "You have to take those kits over there."

I examined the kits. Each kit contained thirty-seven pieces. Bold black letters were stamped on the cardboard packing carton: "Some Assembly Required." On my personal scale of anxiety attacks only the words "Smoking May Be Hazardous to Your Health" rank as high as "Some Assembly Required." My fear and trembling date to early childhood, the Erector Set years. On my eighth birthday my parents gave me an Erector Set and glowed as I assembled a skyscraper. But I had one piece left over. On my second attempt I had one piece too few. Then the skyscraper collapsed. I wanted to give up, but my parents insisted I try once more. I did. Then I flushed the Erector Set down the toilet. One screw at a time. After calling a plumber, my parents took me to a child psychologist. Extensive testing confirmed what I already knew—at birth they forgot to tighten the technological genes. On the other hand I had special talents in animal husbandry.

After the Erector Set trauma I vowed never again to engage in a close encounter with a do-it-yourself project. Until Floyd's Lumber and Mike. "You really think I can figure out how to assemble these chairs?" I asked Mike. The word "assemble" spurred Mike into action. (Like the words "Let us pray" in my profession.) Mike awakened for a third time. Really awakened. Both eyes. Seized in a fit of ecstasy, he jumped onto the stack of Adirondack Chair Kits, opened the instructions, and in a mellow bass voice broke into song.

> *The left leg's connected to the left side.*
> *The right arm's connected to the right leg.*
> *The seat slat's connected to the back slat.*
> *Now hear the word of the instructions.*
> *Your bones, your bones goin' to sit again.*
> *Your bones, your bones goin' to sit again.*
> *Your bones, your bones goin' to sit again.*
> *Goin' to sit on the boards of the Lord. Hey! Hey! Hey!*

I'm not certain why I bought the kits. Maybe because Mike was gearing up for another verse, but now I have everything spread on the basement floor, and Officer Kelly still hasn't found the culprit who stole the hole, and none of the pieces fit together, and Smith's Plumbers went out of business in 1956, so I can't flush the chairs down the toilet. I should have counted the holes at Floyd's Lumber and reported the missing hole to Mike before he went back to sleep, but too late for that.

Fortunately Old Luke passed by carrying his electric drill on its daily outing. "Old Luke, would you drill a hole?" Old Luke obliged. ZZZZZZZ. I had my hole. On the wrong wooden leg. Now I had an extra hole on the right leg. Old Luke apologized, "Sorry, Dan. If I pass anyone who has an extra hole in his left leg I'll send him over. Maybe you can swap." The hole proved to be a precursor of more serious problems. Small screws expected to fit into big holes. A missing slat on the back but a spare seat. And of course none of the pieces lined up. Finally I matched sufficient parts from the ten Adirondack Chair Kits to end up with seven chairs, although one of the chairs tilted sideways because I substituted an armrest for a leg.

Whenever I drive past Floyd's Lumber (turning down the radio to avoid waking Mike), I sneak a look at the model chairs sitting in front of the store. So easy. They seem so easy to put together. But why should they be any easier to assemble than anything else spilling casually out of the carton of my life? Some assembly is always required as I drill and screw and bang my way through the days. How many of us get it all right or line up all the pieces? On the other hand, we have to try. Only Mike, snoring in his Adirondack chair, has the option to sit it out.

29. Biffy and Arnold

~~~❧~~~

In my years on Tripp Street I only remember one dispute—between Old Luke and the young couple Arnold and Biffy. The argument, listed in the *Tripp Street Chronicles* as the NIMBY-NIMFY case, "Not in My Back Yard"–"Not in My Front Yard" began innocently enough. Arnold and Biffy had moved from their penthouse apartment overlooking the East River but missed the river view. Hoping to transport the New York waterfront into the country, they bought a piece of land on the slope of Murphy's Hill below Old Luke's house and hired a landscape architect to design ponds, sprinkler systems, and a marble fountain modeled after Versailles. The interior of the 8,500 square feet called for two bedrooms, eleven bathrooms, and an Olympic-size swimming pool.

At the meeting of the Architectural Review Board one

member asked, "Why eleven bathrooms?" Biffy, cuddling her black water spaniel, explained that she and Arnold owned eleven Jacuzzis and eleven hot tubs. Obviously they needed eleven bathrooms. The ARB agreed but specified that the neon signpost "Biffy and Arnold's East River in the Country" must be reduced in size to six by three feet and the flashing algae-colored letters turned off at midnight. Old Luke, whose ramshackle farmhouse and chicken coop stood on Murphy's Hill a hundred feet above Arnold and Biffy's site, raised a ridiculous objection. "Ain't going to fit into the rural look of Tripp Street." Of course Old Luke was simply being ornery, and the ARB gave Arnold and Biffy a building permit.

Information on construction progress filtered back to us from Teddy, who visited daily. The first week she retrieved a can of Valvoline diesel fuel, and we knew Big Ben's bulldozer was deep into site work. Teddy also brought Ben's lunch—a provolone, ham, salami, and corned beef sandwich on a hard roll, easy on the mustard. The following week Teddy delivered scraps of wood. Wee Willie's Woodworkers were halfway through framing. Teddy brought the remains of Wee Willie's lunch, a slice of mushroom, green pepper, anchovy, and caper pizza. Then Teddy dragged a Bird shingle onto our porch. Roofing was under way. Teddy also deposited Bird's lunch, a barbecued chicken, on our front stoop. We knew construction was entering the final stage when Teddy (in addition to half a Big Mac) brought a bone into the house. On closer inspection the bone proved to be a brass pipe from one of the eleven Jacuzzis. On the night when Teddy ran up the driveway with a giant "B" glowing in her mouth we knew the signpost had been erected: "Biffy and Arnold's East River in the Country." (Whoops, "iffy and Arnold's East River in the Country.") Construction was complete.

The following morning Marion and I paid a courtesy call on Biffy and Arnold, stopping along the way to greet Old Luke. Poor Old Luke. Puffing on his corncob and cursing. Old Luke's family had lived in the area since arriving from England on the good ship *Skunk Cabbage*, a companion ship to the *Mayflower*. Old Luke's great-great-grandfather many times removed, Very Very Old Luke, had come to Tripp Street from London Town in the seventeenth century to escape urban sprawl. In those days the only building was an Indian tepee retirement village. How could Very Very Old Luke have known that one day Biffy and Arnold, whose family arrived in steerage via Ellis Island in 1909, would build an 8,500-square-foot house with two bedrooms and eleven bathrooms on the property below? Now Old Luke looked down on two hundred feet of rooftop.

Marion and I consoled Old Luke before continuing on to Biffy and Arnold's East River in the Country. Arnold, dressed only in a bathing suit, offered us a glass of Perrier, and we settled into a hot tub, where we were joined by Biffy. Handel's Water Suite played softly in the background. Arnold and Biffy loved their house. "With one exception," Arnold moaned. "Look out the front window."

"Why you look out on Old Luke's chicken coop!" I exclaimed. "Right up there on the hill. How quaint!"

Biffy, playing with a rubber ducky in the Jacuzzi, was distraught. "You call that quaint? Looking at Old Luke's chicken coop? Horrible!"

Marion cackled and I scratched my head. "Arnold, you'll get used to the chicken coop, and who knows what the future will hatch." But in my heart I knew that Old Luke and Arnold/Biffy would never adjust, for there are certain times when life is just no good. Whether it is looking up or looking down.

30. Earth Day

The dirt from Tripp Street.

Earth Day.

A number of years ago God stretched out one of His arms and grabbed a handful of earth. Then, without model or mannequin, He stuck one particle of dirt here, another there, and the next thing He knew out popped a two-legged, two-armed, single-headed creature called Man. Adam. Then God said, "See what you can do with a little dirt—if you are resourceful."

Well, times have changed. Most people come into being through less down-to-earth methods, and we have forgotten our origins from a handful of dark rich dirt. A shame. Because, if we knew whence we cometh, we would have a little more respect for the earth, for the ground beneath our feet.

If we knew that Adam, our great-great-great-granddaddy (a

million times removed), might be related to a clump of earth alongside Tripp Street, would we litter his birthplace with a McDonald's Styrofoam carton? Oh, well, how many of us really know our family history! How many of us remember that once upon a time the earth gave us life? If we remembered, we might show the earth respect. A little. Instead of a litter.

And that is why on a spring morning when frogs croaked, buds budded, and mayflies flew, Tripp Street proclaimed an official Earth Day.

The trumpeting sounds of thunder echoed in the morning air, and someone riding on a black cloud dumped a whole lot of water on the area, probably to prepare us for the great cleanup. But then the sun winked through the branches of an oak tree and I wandered out on Tripp Street with paper (recycled) and pen to chronicle the events. Here goes.

First, the deer. Yes, even the deer took part in Earth Day. There was Bambi Baby standing right in the middle of my vegetable patch. I called out, "Hey, eat litter not lettuce!" Bambi Baby looked in my direction, checked her calendar, decided deer-hunting season was still a ways off, and went back to eating. How do you teach a deer to eat what's on the ground, not what grows out of the ground? No respect. Absolutely no respect.

Next, the children. Jason and Jennifer. How cute. Jason wore little white shorts and a blue Polo T-shirt. Just like Daddy. And Jennifer pranced around in a pink party dress. I heard she left Samantha's birthday party early to be part of Tripp Street's Earth Day celebration. The Great Cleanup. Jason and Jennifer stood in front of my house digging up the earth where my new day lilies waved in the morning breeze. Whoops! "No, no, Jennifer. Don't dig up my day lilies!" Too late. Well, the children are only eight. And they are participating in Earth Day, a good omen for the future. Anyway, I can replant the day lily bulbs.

"Jason, Jennifer, please give me back the bulbs!" Jason

wheeled a wheelbarrow partially filled with dirt. My day lily bulbs were in the middle of the pile.

"We're selling dirt," Jennifer announced. "Two shovels for a quarter."

"Selling dirt?"

"Sure," Jason answered. Not missing a beat. "Today is Earth Day. Dad said we could clean up!"

I was sure their father, an investment banker, was only kidding. I was also sure Jason didn't even know the meaning of his words. On the other hand, this was the 1990s.

And my day lily bulbs? Gone. Between Bambi Baby and Jason and Jennifer, Earth Day was off to a lousy start. My little stretch of earth, stripped of the vegetables above the ground and the flowers beneath the ground, would never survive too many Earth Days.

Then I spied Edna and Marguerite, captains of two Garden Club teams dedicated to picking up Tripp Street trash. Edna's team began on the north end of Tripp Street, where skunk cabbages emerge from the swamp. Marguerite began on the south end. They would meet at my house to count litter. The team with the most litter would win a medal inscribed "Outstanding Earthlings." (Marguerite's husband, who conceived the medal, writes scripts for "Star Trek.")

"They're coming!" The cry echoed along Tripp Street, drowning out the sound of Wayne's Jeep Cherokee pulling out of his driveway and spewing exhaust fumes. Throngs of Tripp Streeters (seven to be exact) flocked to my front lawn as the teams converged. Then suddenly a fight broke out.

"That's mine!"

"No, I saw it first!"

And there were Edna and Marguerite threatening to trample my one remaining clump of day lilies as they reached for an empty Gatorade bottle. Would the outcome of the Great Cleanup Contest be decided by a Gatorade bottle? Seemed that way. I offered to throw away another Gatorade bottle (Lemon-

Lime) and even the odds, but my offer was rejected. Soon the E team was shoving the M team, Jennifer and Jason were digging up the last of the day lilies, and Bambi Baby, off to one corner, meditated on humans acting like animals. I returned to the peace of my home and thumbed through the pamphlet entitled *100 Ways to Save the Environment*, searching for a method that did not involve either man or beast. Let us do the littering. Let some other species do the cleaning. No one can be proficient in all aspects of life.

And that brings you up to date on the dirt from Tripp Street.

31. The Spider Web

⟲

"Spider webs don't wait for the wanton wants of man."
(Excerpted from *Natural Occurrences on Tripp Street*, Winding
Road Press.)

. . .

"Welcome to the first in a series of one lecture, 'An Evening
Spent Spinning Spider Stories,' in which we will learn that the
Great Spirit created the spider before any of earth's creatures,
and similar yarns designed to entangle you in spider lore. Our
guest this evening will be Argiope Trifasciata (known by his
intimates as Argy), a banded garden spider who hangs around
between the purple asters and the pink petunias.

"Enter Argy busily at work in the flower garden. Good
Argy. Perched on the pink petunia, releasing a thread of silk.

Caught by a breath of wind. Going, going, gone. Smack onto the purple aster. Stick. That's it, Argy, now crawl across the thread, your golden back bordered with dark stripes. Spin companion threads. Widen your suspension bridge. Whoops! Careful, Argy, you're swaying. Balance, Argy, balance. Cross the bridge. Trail a thread. Create a frame. Strengthen the center. Spin out spokes. Watch it, Argy! Here comes a chickadee. Shame on you, chickadee. Shame. Picking on Argy. Argy lets go of the dragline attached to the web and disappears in the weeds. Danger passes. Will Argy reappear? Sure. There he is! Climbing up the third aster from the right! We're proud of you, Argy! Victory snatched from a chickadee's beak.

"Now, it's dinnertime, Argy. Trap. Trap. Trap. The sun's sinking. What's on the menu, Argy? Fly under thread? Grasshopper wrapped in silk?

"For those unaware of the wonders of spider silk we leave Argy for a moment and journey to distant New Guinea, where native tribes use spider strands as fishing rods, or to a nearby astronomy lab, where the scientist uses spider silk for sighting marks in telescopes. A single spider can generate over 150 yards of silk thread in little more than an hour. My dear friends, please show your admiration for the diverse strands of Argy's life." (Applause fills the lecture hall.)

"Now we return to Argy spinning away from petunia to aster. There, Argy! There! A mosquito bounces onto your sticky web. Uh-oh. Stuck. Sorry, mosquito. Go get it, Argy. Snack time. (Argy crawls over to his prey.) Shlurp. Shlurp. All gone. One mosquito less. One itch less. Yay, Argy!" (More applause in the lecture hall.)

A question from the audience: "Do you have any pictures of Argy's web?"

I hang my head in sadness. "Sir, I am sorry. I planned on giving a slide lecture, but when Argy finished his web the sun was setting and shadows fell on the pink petunias. I decided to wait for the morning to take a picture. So I bid Argy a night of gossamer dreams. She tucked herself into a corner of the web, and I curled up in a feather quilt. In the morning me and my Nikon bounced out the back door to the petunia patch. Now comes the sad part of my story. Overnight someone had ruined Argy's web. The petunias were threadbare. Oh, dear sir. Why didn't I shoot away last night? At sunset. Now it is too late. Too late to do anything but cry over split silk.

"Worse! Much worse! Argy had disappeared. Okay, who swallowed Argy? Chickadees! Confess! Get away from the bird feeder! Not a seed until one of you chirps. Okay, fly to the feeder next door. You'll be back. I have the best food in town. You'll be back.

"Well, folks, that's all there is. End of the lecture. No pictures tonight. I'm sorry. I shouldn't have waited. Never again. By the way, if anyone sees Argy, please send him home. Oh, yes, and remember 'Spider webs don't wait for the wanton wants of man.' (*Natural Occurrences on Tripp Street*, Winding Road Press.) So seize the moment, seize the day, seize the camera."

32. A Redheaded Kid with Freckles

Oh, what a beautiful morning,
Oh, what a beautiful day.
I've got a wonderful ten-speed.
Every bike's going my way.

Helmet fastened, tuna sandwich in hip pack, water bottle full, I coasted down Murphy's Hill on a bicycle trip.

The trees are as high as a woodpecker's eye.
Oh, what a beautiful day!

Onto Route 22, right on 172, horse country. Colts celebrating summer romped in the fields. "Get a bike," I shouted to a white mare. "Get a bike."

Then I saw him. The redheaded kid with freckles. He was

pedaling a three-speed rusty Schwinn and weaving from one
side of the road to the other. Untied yellow shoelaces dragged
on the road, and his pink "I Love NY" sweatshirt billowed in
the breeze. Pulling up to him on my spiffy purple bike, I scoffed,
"Hey, want to be a cyclist? Dress the part!" My chest burst out
of a gold and black spandex shirt, and my thighs rippled beneath knee-length form-fitted green pants. Right out of *Better
Bikes and Riders*.

The kid doffed his Mets cap as I adjusted the rearview
mirror on my helmet.

"Where you going, mister?"

"Pound Ridge," I answered.

"Me too. Want to go together?"

So we went. A male version of Lady and the Tramp. Me on
my state-of-the-art Trek bicycle and the kid on his rusty
Schwinn. As we cycled along Pound Ridge Road the kid
pumped vigorously. I shifted into a lower gear and glided ef-
fortlessly past rambling estates. Then the kid signaled left onto
a dirt road. "Hey, mister, come on this way. A shortcut. Save
you a half hour."

I looked at the road sign. Digby Lane. Unfolding my road
map, I followed the route plotted the night before. Digby Lane?
Not even on the map. "I can't find it, kid." The kid looked.
"Should be here somewhere. Right between Over the Ridge
and Under the Ridge roads. Well don't worry, mister, I take
Digby Lane home from school every day."

"What's the road like?" I asked my redheaded freckled companion.

"A few hills. Not bad. You can make it, mister. Trust me."

I trusted the kid. Why? He was cute. Anyway, who can
turn down a shortcut? Didn't that old Greek Aristotle once say,
"Life is too short to be long." Or was that Yogi Berra?

We were thirty minutes into the trip when we hit Mount
Everest. Okay, I'm exaggerating but the ascent went up and up
and up.

THE DIRT FROM TRIPP STREET

This hill is as high
As a cloud in the sky,
And if I'm not careful
I surely will die!
Oh, what a terrible morning,
Oh, what a terrible day.
I have a terrible feeling
With redheaded kids never play.

The kid left me singing in the dust. With his Schwinn creaking steadily up the hill, he disappeared around a bend. I inched along. Sweat poured into my eyes, and a pickup truck splashed my gold shirt a muddy brown. Then I saw him. The second coming of the redheaded kid with freckles. Pedaling down the hill chewing on a Tootsie Roll. "What happened to you, mister?" How do you strangle a redheaded kid with freckles? Especially when he turns around and races back up the hill. What was he feeding that Schwinn? By this time my left knee throbbed and I grunted in pain every time my foot pushed the pedal. Finally the hill ended. Farmland stretched out before me as far as the eye could see, which was not very far, since a second hill loomed ahead.

On my right, laundry hung on the porch of a worn blue Victorian house where a man dressed in tattered overalls spoke from deep inside a scruffy beard. "Maw, look, it's one of those fancy bike people from down country." Maw rocked steadily back and forth, back and forth, swatting horse flies and spitting out chewing tobacco. "Ain't got nothin' better to do," I heard Maw say as I braced for hill number two on the Digby Lane shortcut.

Hill number two. The mother of all hills. Also the father. Throw in a handful of uncles, aunts, nephews, and nieces. "Redheaded kid with freckles, if I ever catch you prepare to meet your maker!" Halfway up hill number two my bike suffered a puncture, let out a final gasp of air, and wobbled into a ditch. At least the bike knew when to give up. Picking myself out of the ditch, I surveyed the surrounding countryside. There was a large red barn, and on the barn boards a farmer had painted a white sheep above a crossed rod and staff. Next to the sheep were the words "The Lord is my shepherd. Digby Farms 1933."

Was I hallucinating? Had the redheaded kid with freckles sent help from above? The lord is my shepherd! Shame! Shame on you, cyclist of little faith. God, who takes care of lost sheep, will help you gear up (or gear down) to the task ahead. Born again, I changed the tire and continued the grueling task of climbing. Digby Farms stretched on for several miles before I encountered a second barn. This one also had a painted verse: "I shall not want."

Correct, I shall not want to cycle on Digby Lane. Ever again. In this life or in the life to come, which might come very soon, since my heart was racing along at high speed.

I'm not sure how far I pedaled before I arrived at the last of the Digby Farm barns, painted in soothing green, with the words "He maketh me to lie down in green pastures."

Once again the God of Digby Farms spoke to me, and I lay down in Farmer Digby's newly planted cornfields where tiny little cornstalks pushed their silky heads out of the warm earth.

"The corn is as high as a cyclist's right eye." (I always sleep on my right side). "I hope that this journey ends by and by."

When I awoke the sun was setting. I hurried on to Route 137 and called Marion. She had been worried.

"Where have you been for seven hours?"

"Nowhere special. Just out for a bicycle ride."

"Why were you away so long?"

"I found a shortcut."

That bicycle trip on Digby Lane saddled me with two new spokes of understanding on the wheel of life: 1) There are no shortcuts. 2) Never trust a redheaded kid with freckles.

33. SPUD

———⊙———

"**B**ehind every child who digs up potatoes is a mother who has dug up him." (From *The Collected Hodgepodge of Jason of Tripp Street.*)

. . .

Loretta, wife of Garth, mother of Jason, was a founding member of the Northeast Chapter of SPUD, Smothering Parents Ultimately Destroy, a self-help group of overly protective parents. Although Loretta never missed a meeting, SPUD proved ineffective. Loretta continued to smother her child and worry about Jason's every action. For instance, when Jason, Mark, Emily, and Kira were given their first bicycles at the annual Three Wheel Bike Day celebration, Mark, Emily, and Kira pedaled in circles, the approved pattern according to the

Round the Block Nursery School. Not Jason. Jason pedaled in a straight line.

After a sleepless night Loretta brought Jason to Dr. Kidd, the child psychologist at Columbia Presbyterian Hospital. "Jason pedals in a straight line. Will he be all right?" Dr. Kidd smiled and reassured Loretta. "Don't be concerned. Eventually Jason will go in circles. We all do. Just let him be." Loretta couldn't. When Jason came home from nursery school with a drawing of a black bunny, his mother despaired. "Whoever heard of a black bunny?" And she rushed off to the Round the Block Nursery School. "Miss Abigail, I read that when a child uses only one color, especially black, he lacks personality. Is my Jason colorless?"

"Now, Mrs. Barnett," Miss Abigail said, "Jason has a delightful personality. He drew a black bunny because he got to the crayons after everyone else. All the colors were gone."

Loretta breathed a sigh of relief, but then a feeling of dread swept over her. "Why did he get to the crayons last? Is he lacking an aggressive instinct? Should we give Jason karate lessons? He can practice on Emily and Kira."

Loretta increased her attendance at SPUD meetings to four evenings a week, but in March of the first grade Emily read a major work of literature, *Scuffy the Tugboat*. Jason did not read a word until April. "Should we take Jason out of school? Have a tutor? Send him to boarding school? If he is so far behind now, how will he ever get into Harvard?"

Years later, Jason would report in *The Collected Hodgepodge of Jason of Tripp Street:* "Theologically, the sins of the mothers are visited upon the children. Behind every child who digs up potatoes is a mother who has dug up him." Potatoes? What did that have to do with an overly protective mother? A footnote led me to an extensive explanation of Jason's strange comment. For the sake of brevity (Jason's footnote rambles on for forty-seven pages) I will summarize his thought. When Jason was in the second or third grade, he separated from his mother (a wise decision!) and imitated his father. When Garth pulled out of the driveway on his way to work, Jason hastily gathered up his papers (a Peanuts comic strip and two pictures of Teenage Mutant Ninja Turtles) and followed on his three-wheeler. When Garth settled back after dinner and lit a cigar, Jason bit into a Tootsie Roll.

That summer Jason decided to take up gardening. His father was a true gentleman farmer, tending roses, staking tomatoes, spraying apple trees. Jason would be a gentleboy farmer. He pleaded with his dad to give him his own five-by-five-foot patch of land. Garth agreed, and Jason pulled out a row of his father's prize Big Boy Tomatoes, planting them in his square. Unfortunately he left the roots behind. Then the boy announced to his angry father, "Daddy, your tomatoes are living with me."

Regaining his composure, Garth went to the garden center and returned with a potato. Not an ordinary potato. A crusty brown potato with green shoots.

"Jason, plant this potato and soon the sprouts will grow into potato plants. You'll have lots of potatoes."

Garth found a certain poetic justice in teaching his son to grow spuds. Now when Loretta came home from the twice-a-day (as of May 1) SPUD meetings, she and her son would have a common ground.

Too common! Four hours after Jason planted his potato, he dug it up to see if the potato had grown. Disappointed, he stuck the potato back into the ground and waited until the next morning. When his father drove off to work, Jason again uncovered the potato. After all, he had given the shoots twelve hours to become potato plants. Each day, once, maybe twice, Jason dug up his potato. After a week he did notice a change. The green shoots had turned brown. Dejected, he went to his father. "Daddy, look what happened to my potato."

What could Garth do? The boy and his mother came from the same roots. Taking Jason on his lap, he tried to explain.

"Son, potatoes need to grow on their own. You can't keep watching over them or digging them up."

"But I was only helping!" Jason protested.

"I know, son. But potatoes find their own way. In their own time. They'll come up. Just give them a little water, not too much, and let nature do the rest."

Garth gave Jason a new potato, then signed the boy up as a charter member of SPUD Jrs. As Loretta and Jason bundled off to their meeting, Garth shook his head in despair.

34. The Great Takeover

Not long ago Garth and I sat down for a man-to-man talk. About takeovers. Garth, an investment banker, made his name and fortune in the era of mergers and acquisitions. "Yes, Dan, I'm a real success in my profession!" Then his voice trailed off. "Whatever that means."

Listening to Garth's comments on the deals he structured—RJR-Nabisco, GE-RCA, Sony–Columbia Pictures—I wondered how I could hold up my end of the conversation. What did I know about takeovers? Sure, God once took over the world and merged heaven and earth, but that's old stuff. In the '80s and '90s, Monday's headlines are Friday's small print. Then I heard myself say, "Garth, are you familiar with the Great Zucchini Takeover?"

Garth prides himself on knowing corporate history, and I

DANIEL S. WOLK

watched as his analytical mind dredged up material on the Great Zucchini Takeover. "Don't tell me," he said. "Zucchini was the Italian manufacturer who—"

But I shook my head. "Wrong, Garth, wrong." Then, easing myself into his rocking chair with the Harvard Seal, I explained. "Garth, the Great Zucchini Takeover began in early March with the manure."

"Manure?"

"That's right. How can you plant zucchini unless you dump manure on your garden?" Garth moaned. Another one of my gardening stories. "Every day after work I stopped by the stable, picked up several bags of horse manure, and dumped them in my garden." I laughed. "One Saturday I forgot the bags were in the Toyota and drove into New York to the Pierre for a wedding. Me, my tux, and my manure. The doorman who parked the car suggested I check the catalytic converter. 'Strange smell coming out of your car, sir.'

"By late May I had dark rich soil and on Memorial Day planted two types of zucchini seeds. Black Magic (noted for their mystical qualities) and Spineless Beauties. Marion questioned my wretched excess. 'Why do you need so many. Why is two always better than one?'

"How could Marion know the hidden desire lurking in my ego: to be CEO of the largest zucchini crop on Tripp Street. And I was! By mid-June the zucchini plants battled with one another for space, the weaker growth falling by the garden side. Marion felt sorry for a row of zucchini about to be snuffed out by the competition and asked me to intervene. 'Dan, they can't survive without outside support. Help them!' But that's not the way of the world, is it, Garth? Expand! Expand! May the best zucchini win!"

Garth didn't give a hill of beans about gardening matters. Concentrating on the computer in his study, he watched stock prices race across the screen. Undaunted I continued. "By late

June, zucchini blossoms cast a sheet of yellow on the garden, and by early July, Black Magics and Spineless Beauties crept out from under the leaves." Garth looked at his watch and reached for the *Wall Street Journal.*

"Wait, Garth, I'm at the takeover part of the story. The point when the Spineless Beauties went wild. Spineless. Ha! Over hill and dale they left their creeping trail as the Spineless went crawling along. Soon the vines filled the garden and embarked on a hostile takeover. First they raided the parsley and threatened to move on the carrots, who were forced underground. One recluse zucchini hid under a leaf, grew to four pounds, and threatened to squash its next-door squash. Can you imagine? Even among themselves every zucchini was out for itself.

"By mid-July I averaged forty zucchini a day. In the evenings I made my way from home to home giving away zucchini. Yes, I was a familiar sight pushing an A&P shopping cart filled with zucchini up Tripp Street. I also became a nuisance. After a while no one wanted my zucchini, and when they saw me approach lights went off and window shades were pulled down. 'Please,' I cried out, 'my shopping cart runneth over, please share in my success.' Success? In the meantime my garden lacked even a sprig of parsley or a head of lettuce. Vanquished by the Great Zucchini Takeover. Is this what success is all about? Having so many zucchinis? Why, Garth? Why? Why did I succumb to zucchini greed? Why did I think CEO of the largest zucchini patch on Tripp Street would bring me happiness?"

Sadness spread over Garth's face as he rested his head on his computer. "I know what you mean, Dan. RJR-Nabisco, GE-RCA, Sony-Columbia—my illustrious past. And am I more content than when I first started out? When I was on the manure level? Am I?"

"Garth," I reflected, "a wise man once cautioned that 'success is getting what you want. Happiness is wanting what you get.' What do you think, Garth?" My friend didn't reply. Instead he stared out the window, where a zucchini vine, escaped from my garden, climbed the side of his house and wrapped itself around the television antenna. So we sat there, Garth and I, having a man-to-man talk. About takeovers.

35. Jason, Butterfly Hunter

"Happiness is a black and yellow butterfly." (From *The Collected Hodgepodge of Jason of Tripp Street.*)

. . .

On his eighth birthday Jason's parents gave him a designer butterfly net from the Fifth Avenue boutique Butterflies and Things. Would catching butterflies be one more of Jason's flights of fancy? But tell me, what parent can deny a son's request for a butterfly net? Jason pleaded, "Please, Mommy and Daddy, please. I'll be so happy." And who can refuse to grant happiness? If Jason's parents denied his request they might inflict emotional problems on their son. Consider. Jason, twenty years from now, on a psychiatrist's couch. "When I was eight I wished to collect lepidoptera, the common butterfly, but my parents objected. Could that be the reason for my unhappiness? Am I still caught in their net of rejection?" Aware of the potential danger, Garth and Loretta bought Jason a butterfly net, and the boy flew off in pursuit of happiness.

First, he sought out Barry, the butterfly collector who had recently published a scholarly article in the weekly journal of the Butterfly Association of Northern Lichtenstein, "Tripp Street Butterfly Sightings from March 3, 1857–April 16, 1989." Giving generously of his time, Barry instructed Jason on the finer points of butterfly collecting, i.e., what they look like and which end of the net to hold. He even loaned the boy his Berlitz phrase book on butterfly dialects of the Northeast. Sonya, our resident poet, whose saga of life on Tripp Street, *Grubs, Borers, and Skunks,* was required reading at Hickory Branch Elementary School and Harvard University, composed a poem for Jason.

> *Butterflies are red,*
> *Butterflies are blue.*
> *They have many colors,*
> *And happiness does too.*

I was home the day Jason set off on his search for a butterfly. Slogging through the wetlands where Sam the horse was buried in 1909, Jason bumped into a flock of gypsy moths gorging themselves at a maple leaf buffet. Jason had little interest in overstuffed moths. He was after yellow and black Monarchs. But they had little interest in Jason. An hour passed, and Jason rested on a rock by my house. A tear snuck out of the corner of his eye. "I'll never find a butterfly!" he cried.

Just then I spotted a fuzzy little, furry little, brown and orange caterpillar trekking from a clump of skunk cabbage to a distant wild grapevine. Patting Jason on his head, I said, "Take this caterpillar home. In a few days it will hatch into a butterfly. I promise." But Jason couldn't wait that long for happiness. He wanted it now. "Jason, happiness comes slowly," I explained. But Jason didn't hear. Next thing I knew, the boy had spotted a yellow butterfly on the roof of Old Luke's tool shed. Jason waved his net, but he couldn't reach the butterfly. Poor Jason. Happiness, just beyond his grasp. "Please," he cried, "lift me up." But even on another person's shoulders Jason couldn't reach. "Jason, you better find a butterfly on your own level."

Then a velvet black butterfly, accompanied by a gray and red friend, descended on the meadow and zigzagged between blades of grass. Jason gave chase. The black butterfly alighted in a muddy puddle and Jason's net churned the water. "I got it! I got it!" But when he looked into the net all Jason found was a broken twig and two pebbles. Overhead the gray and red butterfly taunted the child. Jason lunged for this butterfly, slipped, and fell into the mud puddle.

Defeated, Jason curled up under a honeysuckle bush and unwrapped a peanut butter and jelly sandwich. Tears dripped down his muddy face and landed in his lap, meeting a blob of strawberry jam. Suddenly a black and yellow butterfly settled on Jason's shoulder. At first the child didn't see it, but when he wiped the peanut butter off his mouth with the back of his hand, Jason discovered the butterfly. Quietly, Jason raised his hand, seized the butterfly and dropped it into a bottle. He looked at his treasure for many minutes, then, in an act of compassion, opened the top, and the butterfly flew off into a field of black-eyed Susans. But, oh, the happiness of those moments!

Years later, when *The Collected Hodgepodge of Jason of Tripp Street* made the best-seller list, "Good Morning America," and won the National Book Award, I read Jason's chapter "On Happiness and the Zen of Butterflies." "Happiness is a black and yellow butterfly. Run after the butterfly, and it may elude your grasp. Sit down, wait, and it may alight upon you."

36. Bambi Baby

When I lost Bambi, I lost the last of my childhood heroes. Of course I didn't really lose Bambi, only the Disneyesque image of the animals we love to love. Bambi still lives and lurks in the shadows of the field across from my house. She and the rest of the Tripp Street Deer Herd wait for the moment when they can devour my garden. In early morning Bambi Baby leaps over my stone wall for breakfast of hosta garnished with a touch of white tulip. Back again in evening, she gobbles up Foie de Rhododendron and Apple Blossom Delight. Oh, dear, my garden's in ruin and Bambi has driven me to song:

> *Doe, a deer, a female deer.*
> *Hey, I wish I had a gun.*
> *Gee, why does she pick on me?*

Fa, I want her on the run.
So, a needle in her head.
La, a curse to follow so.
Tea, I'd cook her in a pot.
That will bring us back to Doe, Hey, Gee, Gee.

There was a time when I thought I could change the eating pattern of the deer. I experimented with a deer I named "Socrates Hooked on Hemlock." Twice a day Socrates wove through my line of hemlock trees shearing the bottom branches. Deer become addicted to hemlock, and a hemlock fix fixed several of my finest trees. Socrates mainlined hemlock. I put out a salt lick, hoping the deer would buck the habit. Failure. I hung "Just Say No" signs on the hemlock trees and when that failed substituted sexually implicit signs, "Just Play Doe." Wasted. Worse, yesterday Socrates brought Felicity Fawn to nibble on my hemlock. Can you imagine, a descendant of Disney's Deer pushing drugs? Corrupting minors? A comforting thought: Soon I'll run out of hemlock, and Socrates will be forced to take to other streets. Nonsense! Yesterday a truck from Brandywine Nursery pulled into my driveway with a truckload of eight-foot hemlock trees. "You Wolk? We have an order here from a Socrates B. Deer. Said to charge it to your account."

If that weren't sufficient to needle me, one eight-point buck carouses wearing a sign "Hill and Dale Nursery." Although I lack proof, I believe Hill and Dale hires deer to eat up gardens and create business. Dale Hill, the owner of Hill and Dale, denies wrongdoing, but I am suspicious. For instance, last week Hill and Dale advertised in our local newspaper, the *Patent Trader:* "Our mistake is your bonanza. We overordered pachysandra and offer a 10 percent discount on purchases of a dozen or more plants." The one thing we don't need on Tripp Street is pachysandra. The stuff covers half the street, and you can't even give it away. But the night the ad appeared the entire deer herd went on a rampage and gorged themselves on pachysandra. Tripp Street was eaten down to the roots. A coincidence? Nonsense! The following afternoon a Hill and Dale truck backed into the deer meadow and dropped off thirty pounds of salt licks. The nursery was paying off the deer. Giving them a lick back.

At this point you might ask, "Why don't the residents of Tripp Street organize to counter deer demolition teams?" We have. The best minds on Tripp Street met and we devised ingenious solutions.

First, I tried scattering human hair around trees and bushes. According to experts, the scent tricks deer into believing humans are nearby, and deer do not want to be close to humans. I should have questioned this approach when two deer stood about ten feet away, watching as I scattered hair. Then, as soon as I disappeared, the largest buck on the street, Jack the Clipper, gave my ewe a crewcut. My second attempt involved covering the trees with a protective netting, but accidentally I trapped myself inside the net and had to negotiate with a deer to slice the net with his antlers in return for one boxwood and a Ballerina rosebush. As of this writing the deer continue to reign.

And I? I have lost my garden. And my childhood hero, Bambi. For that gentle deer, remembered in living color, represented the innocence of youth we would hold forever. If we could. But I have learned. The wonderful world of Disney only exists in reruns on the giant screen of memory, not on the morning reruns of a deer herd through my backyard.

37. A Mountain Ash and a Hemlock

─────◎─────

Three years ago I bought a mountain ash. Most people can't understand why I would want to plant a mountain ash. "That's an old-time tree," the nursery said. "We don't have much of a demand for them anymore." He was correct. The last mountain ash I knew intimately was when I turned sixteen, the age of maturity.

What event marks the passage from boyhood to maturity? Ask any red-blooded American boy and the answer is universal. Driving a car. Why should I be an exception? What a glorious day! The day I received my driver's license! My parents stood in the bay window of our home on South Main Avenue as I backed confidently out of the driveway. Dad had presided at the key-turning-over ceremony. He invoked the traditional prayer for one starting out on the road: "May God bless your going out

and your coming in. Coming in. Coming in, Coming in."
Obviously the return trip loomed larger in my father's mind. I
responded by turning up the car radio to an appropriate song,
"The Battle Hymn of the Republic." "Mine eyes have seen the
glory of the coming of the Ford." Unfortunately, the Ford failed
to see the coming of the thirty-foot mountain ash parked per-
manently in the middle of our front lawn. When the results
were in, the tree claimed a deep scar and the car a dented
fender.

I also acquired a fondness for mountain ash and promised
myself that someday I would plant a mountain ash of my own.
When my personal odometer reached fifty, I turned over the
ground, erected a sign, "Future Home of the Mountain Ash,"
and encouraged Teddy to do her part in fertilizing the spot. In
April a notice arrived from the Newton Seed Company announcing the shipment of the mountain ash. Alerting UPS to
place a larger truck on the route, I cleared out the garage and
waited. Tax day the tree arrived in a two-foot-long package.
"Tree's here," Jim of UPS called.

"Impossible. I'm expecting a mountain ash. The carton's
too small."

Jim shrugged. "Maybe they're sending one branch at a
time!"

A sixteen-inch seedling packed in a moist plastic bag lay
inside the carton. Carrying the tree out to its home, I saw a
family of finches who had planned to nest in the branches fly off
in search of bigger quarters. Another failed real estate deal!
Also, the five-foot-wide and three-foot-deep hole I had dug was
too large. After spreading the roots in their new home, I filled
in the hole and replaced my "Future Home of the Mountain
Ash" sign with a series of red directional arrows from the garage
to the tree. Otherwise I might lose the seedling.

Three years have passed since the mountain ash took root
on Tripp Street. The tree measured three feet, eight inches on
its third birthday and numbered a half dozen red berries. Within

fifty years the mountain ash may be as large as the original tree on South Main Avenue. Unfortunately, an event yesterday afternoon could traumatize my tree and stunt future growth. I am referring to the orange bulldozer that clunked off a flatbed and made a break in the stone wall across the way. As a Tripp Street chronicler, I monitor every unusual event occurring in the neighborhood. Waving my hands, I confronted the driver, a burly man named Red who greeted my interference by calmly crushing a Budweiser beer can and flicking it off my head. "What are you doing?" I called. "Subdividing," he answered. "What's it to you, buddy?" And he pointed a hairy arm in my direction. Before I could reply he aimed the bulldozer at a seventy-foot hemlock, pushed on the throttle, and headed toward the evergreen. For the first time in thirty-five years I understood how my parents felt when they watched me back into the mountain ash. With one exception. They were worried about the Ford. I was worried about the stately hemlock casting shade on generations of passersby and contributing a soft bed of pine needles for Jason and his friends. Too late. Big Red on Bull Dozer had made contact with the evergreen. A groan echoed from the bowels of the earth and a redheaded woodpecker flew to safety. The hemlock crashed to the earth, felled by Big Red, who shouted in my direction as he backed his tractor onto the flatbed. "All done, buddy. All done."

The air was still as I returned home, but my three-foot, eight-inch mountain ash quivered. It had seen the death of the hemlock. Even a shot of Miracle Grow failed to calm its nerves. "Is this all there is to life?" the tree whispered in the evening breeze. "To grow, only to be pushed down?" How could I comfort the mountain ash? When you get to the root of the matter, life is like that. The years pass and we emerge into maturity, slowly spreading our limbs into space. But in a brief second we are cut down. Why?

The mountain ash had no answer. The once mighty hemlock could not answer.

38. Jason Runs Away

~⊙~

At 4:18 P.M. on Tuesday, July 23, Jason ran away from home. Loretta, Jason's mother, was walking Applegate, the family poodle. She walked Applegate every day from 4:03 to 4:33, and Jason seized the moment when Loretta was farthest away to plan the Great Escape. Loretta and Garth should have sensed Jason's intentions. Hadn't he warned them? "Mom, Dad, I'm eight years old now. My allowance is only forty-nine cents [yearly increments of seven cents per year], and I have to go to bed at eight. It's not fair." Garth had patted Jason on the head and said, "Well, son." Loretta hugged her oldest child and added, "Now, dear." Then the parents dismissed the issue. Not Jason. He would run away. Mary had run away for over two hours in September. Eric had made it as far as Route 143 in May. What Tripp Street kid doesn't run away from home at

least once? And what better reason than a forty-nine-cent allowance and an 8:00 P.M. curfew? Justice fell on Jason's side!

The night before, Jason had packed his chartreuse canvas
book bag. What did he pack? Well, if you were planning to run
away from home what would you consider? The essentials of
life.

For physical sustenance: peanut butter on celery and Chips
Ahoy. For security: GI Joe. For a friend: Bertram, the stuffed
bunny. For a tie with the past: Blanky, the pink blanket Jason
sucked for five and a half years.

Transportation was to be provided by his loyal bicycle, Big
Wheel.

With the exception of neglecting to pack the peanut butter
on celery in a Baggie (thereby leaving a peanut butter stain on
GI Joe and Bertram Bunny's nose), Jason was well prepared for
the hostile environs beyond Tripp Street. At 4:18 P.M., burst-
ing with confidence, Jason headed off to make his way in the
world.

Loretta discovered Jason's disappearance when she found
the open peanut butter jar in the kitchen. Stuffed inside was his
note: "Dear Mom and Dad. I rund a waay. Luv Jason."

"Come, Applegate," Loretta called. "We have to find Jason." Applegate, glad to get Jason out of the house and with
designs on the boy's room, had curled up on the sofa. Loretta
drove down Tripp Street and onto Heather Place. In the distance a child splashed in a puddle, and Loretta bounced along
the rough road. "Jason! Jason!" But it was only Greg from
Greenwood Drive. Oh, how cute, Loretta thought, as Greg's
white shorts and yellow sweatshirt turned muddy brown. And
then Jason's mother remembered how she had scolded Jason for
playing in a puddle. Just two days ago. Oh! Was that why Jason
had run away? If he comes home I'll buy him the biggest mud
puddle. Just for my Jason. A Hammacher Schlemmer mud puddle. And I'll never yell at him again. Never! (Personal aside.
The reader knows Loretta will renege on her promise once

Jason returns. At the very most she will buy him a tiny cheap mud puddle from Puddles "R" Us. And as far as never yelling at Jason again? Come now, Loretta!)

Meanwhile, back on Big Wheel, Jason had cut through Old Luke's property, following the ridge path where at night coyotes howl and the last of the mighty Algonquins smoke their peace pipes and consider a strategy to buy back Manhattan Island from the Japanese. Then he descends onto Jingle Lane, free at last! Yes, Loretta and Garth, Jason's free at last!

Our story returns to Loretta, who has turned on the windshield wipers of her BMW, only to discover that the day is bright and sunny but she is crying. Returning home, she curls up on the sofa next to Applegate, still snoring away, and calls Garth at the office. To her dismay Garth has also run away. Mildred, Garth's secretary, informs Loretta, "Your husband said if it was important he could be reached on the squash court. Is it important?"

"Important?" Loretta cried. "Important? Jason ran away from home. If your son ran away wouldn't you be desperate?"

At the other end of the phone Mildred laughed. "My son's twenty-seven and still living at home. I only wish he'd run away!"

When Loretta finally reached Garth, he informed her that he had beaten the second seed at the club. "What a day," he panted. "What a day! I qualified for the Easterns."

Loretta sniffled at the other end of the phone. "Oh, Garth, it's a terrible day."

"Don't worry, dear. I'll only be at the championship for one night. Then I'll be home. Don't cry."

"Garth," Loretta sobbed, "Jason ran away from home. I found a note in the peanut butter jar."

"How long ago?" Garth asked.

"Almost a half hour. When I was walking Applegate."

"Couldn't you find him in the car?"

"No, I drove all over. I thought Greg was Jason. Greg

looked so cute. But I couldn't find Jason. And he hasn't called. Or written. What happens if he starves, or one of the ducks on Heron Pond attacks him? Garth, please come home."

"Now, Loretta, calm down. I'm sure he'll be back soon. It'll be all right," Garth comforted.

"How do you know he'll come home?" Loretta cried. "Mary ran away for two hours, and when they found Eric he had a scraped knee, and when Roger walked out on Lydia he never came home, and did Max's grandfather come back after he died and—"

"Loretta, I'll be on the 6:03. By the time I'm home I just bet Jason will be wheeling in on Big Wheel. Try to relax. Turn on Oprah or Donahue. Everything will be all right. I love you."

Garth was right. Jason returned at 5:14, when he remembered his mother had baked chocolate brownies for dessert. Chocolate fudge brownies. Applegate, realizing he was back in the doghouse, took his bone out of Jason's room. Loretta squeezed Jason, kissed him, and cried.

"Jason, Jason, my darling. How I love you. I never realized how much I love you."

And probably we never do know how much we love someone until we realize we may lose them. Until we realize we may lose them.

39. A Stone by the Side of the Road

What do you see when you see a stone wall?

Old Luke sees the past, when his grandparents worked the land. "Those two walls running parallel to each other along your driveway, they were a cow run. Turn-of-the-century farmers like my granddad herded cows from barn to pasture and back again along the path."

Ollie, the neighborhood historian, smiles whenever he looks down towards Crooks Notch, where a wavy stone wall marks our property line. "That's a whiskey wall."

"What's a whiskey wall?" I asked Ollie.

"In the old days there were a lot of lazy wall builders. The foreman put a jug of whiskey fifteen or twenty feet down the field. When the workmen reached that point they could drink the whiskey. The rest of the day they staggered. So did the wall!"

Mrs. Martha Parsons loves the wide stepping-stone in the front wall. In the nineteenth century ladies in flowing petticoats descended from a stagecoach onto this flat stepping-stone and made their way across the lawn. After struggling with the rough-hewn stone steps leading up from the road, I suggested to Mrs. Parsons, "You don't have to come by horse to use the stepping-stone." Now Mrs. Parsons's ninety-horsepower Ford Pinto drives up to the stone.

Only Joyce seemed unimpressed with our stone walls. I was surprised. Joyce loved horses. She spent winters riding in Palm Beach and summers in Bedford. I thought she would like the iron rings for hitching horses set into the stone wall. How many homes offer hitching posts? "Joyce, why don't you ride over on Mr. Granddaddy? Tie him up here." I pointed to a stone. Joyce shook her head and bent down near a fieldstone lying alongside the road. The stone, loosened by the spreading roots of a lilac bush, had fallen off the wall.

"Why don't you put this stone back in place?" she asked.

"Joyce, that stone weighs several hundred pounds. I couldn't lift it if I wanted to. Why worry about a single stone when you have an entire wall to admire?"

Joyce tried to lift the stone, then she turned to me and whispered sadly, "The poor stone."

In a feeble attempt to lighten the mood I said, "Joyce, it's one thing not to move a stone, but to be moved by a stone?" She rose slowly. "Dan, please. I know it's ridiculous to care about a stone, but ever since the divorce . . ." Joyce and Frank had agreed to the divorce in early January. No fighting. Joint custody. Both independently wealthy. They had been married for nineteen years, after meeting at the University of North Carolina. The perfect marriage. Eventually they grew apart. Then the divorce. At first Joyce loved the freedom. Her days were filled as a vice president at Flater and Schultz, hosting benefits for the Met, the Whitney, the Heart Fund. Courted by New York society, she flew off to Paris or St. Martin for long weekends with Fortune 500 men. No one worried about Joyce. Except Joyce.

"Dan, last week Carol asked me to go with her to one of those sensitivity workshops in New York. Can you imagine me at a sensitivity workshop?" Joyce laughed. "But I went. The facilitator was a gaunt man with a shaggy beard and a black turtleneck. Hardly my taste. We went through a series of 'getting to know you' exercises, and then he asked, 'When I say pen what do you think of?' My friend Carol answered, 'I think of a felt tip.' Someone named Natalie said, 'Ink spots on my white dress.' Finally he turned to me. 'Joyce?' At first I hesitated, then I heard myself saying, 'When I hear the word pen, I think of a pencil. A pen and pencil. A complete set. A man and a woman. To love and be loved.' Then I turned red from embarrassment."

Joyce and I were silent for a moment. Then we bent over and put the stone back in place. "Dan," Joyce sighed. "When I look back at my divorce I'm not certain what went wrong. Maybe I thought too much about myself. Maybe Frank did. Who knows. But for the first time I realize I do not want to be alone. Disconnected from the world. I do not want to be a stone by the side of the road. And next time—"

Joyce's voice broke off, but I knew what she was thinking. Next time, and there would be a next time, in love, in friendship, she would reach out, share, and be joined to the wall of existence.

40. The Boomerang

———⟲———

Jason lost his faith in God when he lost his boomerang. Historians are uncertain when he discovered his faith in God, but he lost it when he lost his boomerang. At the age of eight.

In the years when Jason was still a believer we would sit under the sugar maple and talk boomerangs. "Jason, did you know boomerangs have been around a long, long time? Someone told me the first boomerang came from Australia fifteen thousand years ago."

My eight-year-old friend asked, "How long is that?"

"Well, Jason, that's before koala bears. Even before Qantas."

And so we sat under the maple tree, Jason and I, bringing back the past, bringing back Silky Spinner, an oak boomerang. Jason would let Silky fly into the sun, followed by Teddy, who thought she was chasing a stick. There they go. Silky cutting the air with a boomerang hum, Teddy trampling the lettuce, jumping junipers in hot pursuit. I can't be sure, but if Jason lost his faith in God when he lost his boomerang, Teddy lost her faith in sticks, when, instead of landing at Teddy's feet Silky returned to Jason's hand. Poor Teddy. Like chasing her tail.

Jason dreamed of the day he would catch a boomerang behind his back. "Thirty-seven times without a miss, that's the record!" He also read of a boomeranger who knocked an apple off his own head. And one clear night when a crescent moon rose over the fields, I explained to Jason, "That's the boomerang of all boomerangs, off on a round-the-world journey. Back in a month."

One summer morning over lemonade, Jason and I carved a birch-wood boomerang and decorated the surface with red, white, and blue stripes. An All-American Australian boomerang. A light breeze blew in from the northeast as we launched the boomerang. Boomer hit the air current, dipped up and down, and flew home, completing its maiden journey with dignity and grace.

"Jason," I asked, "any idea why the boomerang returns?" Before Jason could answer I let fly with my intensive research into boomerangiana. "Boomeranging combines the Bernoulli Principle and Newton's laws of motion and gyroscopic stability. What do you think?"

Jason rose to his full eight-year-old stature, looked me straight in the eye, and answered, "You're wrong."

"Wrong? With big names like Bernoulli, Newton, and gyroscopic you call me wrong? Well then, how do you think the boomerang returns?"

Jason took a sip of lemonade before condescending to answer. "I throw the boomerang out. God throws the boomerang back."

"God?"

"Uh-huh. We're having a catch. God and me. You should know that. God's your business."

"Okay, Jason. You're right. You and God are partners. Not bad. But tell me, is God right-handed or left-handed?"

Jason scoffed.

August passed. Quiet months of boomeranging. Then one morning, the Monday of July Fourth weekend if my memory is correct, Jason stopped by. Boomerangless.

"Where's the boomerang?" I shouted.

Jason shoved his hands into the pockets of his shorts and shrugged. "Don't know."

"Don't know?"

"Lost. God didn't throw it back. He doesn't want to play with me anymore. I don't care. I won't play with Him anymore!"

A tear dripped into Jason's lemonade. What could I do? How could I comfort a child who lost his boomerang and his God? Only one approach! The truth.

"Jason, I know how you feel. You're ready to play, but not everyone else is, especially not God. God's busy at this time of year—planning heat waves, thunderstorms, July Fourth celebrations. I'm sure God loves playing boomerang with you, but God has a full schedule."

Jason rejected the boomerang theory of God.

"If God cared, God would have thrown it back. I know."

Yes, Jason, I thought, we expect a lot from others. Even from God. But sometimes the boomerang flies a solitary route with no one at the receiving end. Sometimes, Jason, sometimes we have to do it by ourselves, rely on our own resources. Living. Losing. Finding. Boomeranging.

Autumn

41. Recycling Day

———◎———

Last Thursday, Recycling Day, Henry and I shared a few thoughts. We were sitting at the foot of our driveways, Henry on a blue bag filled with bottles for the recycling center and I on a pile of newspapers. Between us a raccoon busily poked through the eatable garbage, occasionally lifting up his masked face to catch a bit of gossip.

Henry wasn't really gossiping. He was extolling Recycling Day. "This was one of the reasons I moved out of the city: the thrill of listening to chirping chickadees, breathing the country air, dragging my garbage down the driveway instead of dumping it into the sooty incinerator shaft at 330 East Seventy-fourth Street." Henry doesn't really drag his garbage down the driveway. He loads the garbage into the back seat of his 1990 forest-green Jaguar and escorts his garbage before catching the 8:03 to

Grand Central. But as we sat on our piles of bottles and papers, Henry, dressed in a gray three-piece Ralph Lauren suit, confessed a second reason for moving to Tripp Street, even more profound than garbage, if that is possible. "I wanted to see more of Billy. My son means everything to me. Didn't see much of him in the city. I'd leave for work at 6:30 A.M. and come home at nine or ten. So I decided to move out here, catch the 8:03, leave work early, take off weekends. From now on I'm going to keep up with Old Luke instead of old New York."

To prove this new philosophy Henry pointed to his 1990 Jaguar. "See that car, Dan? The ninety-one Jaguar's already out and I haven't traded in my ninety. Nope. I'm waiting until the ninety-twos. Keeping my car for two years now. How's that for a change in values!" Bandito the Raccoon, impressed with Henry's words, looked up from a pile of chicken bones.

Henry and I set about separating garbage for the recycling bins. Since the day Max, chairperson of the Tripp Street Has Bin Committee, went public with the motto "The Street That Recycles Together, Recycles Together," rubbish was all we thought about. Even Teddy joined the common effort, eating Styrofoam cups from the construction site instead of depositing this environmental menace on our front lawn. However, on this morning Teddy and Bandito watched as Henry and I piled up plastic bottles, tin cans, last week's *New York Times*. Soon the piles stretched across Tripp Street. Max, driving his pickup, stopped on the northern side of the barricade; Lydia in her Saab pulled up on the southern side. On most streets a traffic jam would spawn horn blowing and curses. Not on Tripp Street. Instead Max and Lydia rushed out of their cars to help. Henry shook his head in amazement.

"At 330 East Seventy-fourth Street if anyone caused a bottleneck at the incinerator you could have a riot. One day Sybil stood there reading each section of the Sunday *Times* before throwing it away. Archie, next in line, almost threw Sybil (who weighed ninety-four pounds after her Awful Slim Diet) down the chute. But not on Tripp Street."

Just as we finished, Henry's son, Billy, pulled out of the driveway in Henry's antique 1989 Jag and tossed a plastic Coke bottle onto Tripp Street. Henry was furious and called after the boy, "Billy, don't litter! Americans use two and a half million plastic bottles every hour. What if they threw all of them onto the streets of America!" Billy screeched to a stop, picked up the empty Coke bottle, and gave his father one of those "cool it, Dad" smiles.

Henry calmed down. "Son, didn't mean to yell at you, but concern with the environment's crucial. How about coming with me to the weekly meeting of the Has Bin Committee? We could share a common interest. Wouldn't that be fun?"

Billy got back into the Jaguar and looked at his father. "Can't do it this week, Dad. Too busy. Maybe later. See you." And he drove off down Tripp Street crunching a pile of chicken bones left over from Bandito. Henry slumped against the stone wall.

"I've heard those words before. 'Too busy. Maybe later.' I said them when Billy pleaded with me to sail boats in Central Park, to see him in *Peter Pan*. But I was traveling or at the office. Too busy. Maybe next week. God, I wish I had that time back!"

While Henry tied one of the recycling bags, I remembered a flyer on objects unsuitable for recycling: motor oil, light bulbs, spray cans, lead batteries. But the list left off one item. The most important. You can't recycle time. Sorry, Henry. You can't recycle time.

42. 9:00 P.M. Comes Too Early

⟿

This is the first year my apple tree produced apples. Correction. An apple. A Macintosh. The only one to hang on after the June windstorm. But I'm not discouraged. The tree is still young. In several years I should be handing out apples from one end of Tripp Street to the other. Anyway, the tree has borne other fruit. For instance, my son Scott and I have a new contact point. Scott, a computer expert, always talked about his Apple computer, a Mac II. Now we also talk about my Mac I. Out there in the orchard.

And the tree also sows seeds of memory. Of my mother. Whenever I think of apples I think of my mother. She loved Macs or russets or Jonathans. It didn't matter, as long as it was an apple. Her favorite time for eating apples was 11:00 P.M. just before she went to bed. She would sit in a beige wing chair, her feet resting on a footstool, and the crunch of a crisp apple filled the house.

My father sat at his desk writing sermons, and Hoppy, the black and white Boston terrier, raced from one end of the room to the other, braking at the final second and avoiding a near fatal concussion. Only the crunching of my mother's apple disturbed the peace of our house on South Main Avenue, and biting into a Northern Spy or a Macintosh can hardly be called disturbing the peace. When the swamp maples turned red every autumn, my parents made a pilgrimage to Indian Ladder Farms to buy apples. She stored the apples in the cool attic, and they lasted through winter and spring. Apples usually don't last that long, but I am convinced the apples knew my mother loved them, and the fruit reciprocated by remaining solidly behind her.

When my father died, and my mother moved to a small apartment, the temperature was too high and the apples did not last; but her legendary tie with Macs and Spies and Macouns had long since traveled through the annals of Albany. When she was down to her last apple, a neighbor miraculously appeared with a fresh batch. By this time my mother was in her eighties, but she still sat in her wing chair (re-covered in yellow), a brown and orange afghan draped over her legs, and at 11:00 P.M. ate her apple. The eleven o'clock news invaded her world, but she was more punctual than the news. "Set your clock by Mary Wolk's apple." Eleven bites. Eleven o'clock.

At the age of eighty-six the first in a series of minor strokes confined Mother to her apartment and necessitated full-time help. I interviewed prospective home aides. "Have you worked with the elderly?" "If there were an emergency, what would you do?" "Do you have references?" The standard questions. But the only information I valued was an aide's capacity for empathy. If she cared, if she could see my mother as she might see her own mother. Empathy. And a final concern unique to this special case: "Did the help like apples?" Not that a prior record of apple eating was crucial to employment, only an openness to apple eating. In the next two years my mother converted an entire segment of Albany's nursing population to a love of apples. She was an apple missionary to the very core! Occasionally a dispute arose. Betty, for example, insisted on eating Macouns when they were already out of season and everyone knew Golden Delicious was the correct choice. My mother argued unsuccessfully with Betty. Finally Mother accepted Betty for what she was: a well-meaning soul who ate apples but was your basic apple illiterate. So, at 11:00 P.M., Mother and Betty settled into the two wing chairs, drew out their apples, and with the cacophony of Macouns and Delicious filled the apartment with the sounds of autumn.

It was Grace who changed the format. Grace tended to my mother's needs with consummate care. She was the one who took my mother to Cape Cod for a week. I have the photographs of Mother, age eighty-eight, sitting on the beach in mid-October, bundled from head to toe in a blanket. Grace and my mother became companions; they traveled to the mineral baths in Saratoga (not to take the baths, only to see the bathers), dined at New England inns, attended the Albany Symphony.

Then one day I received a frantic call from my mother. "Grace wants me to go to bed at nine P.M." The call signaled a crisis. I canceled afternoon appointments in New York and rushed upstate. I knew the gravity of that call. My mother had never gone to bed before 11:00 P.M., not even when she was sick. Not my mother. At 11:00 P.M. After her apple. Family research assures me that even in her teen years she refused to retire before 11:00 P.M. (Unfortunately I have been unable to trace this phenomenon into the early formula years, but I imagine even then she rocked around in her crib until 11:00 P.M., retiring only after her mother coaxed her to sleep with applesauce. This of course is conjecture.)

When I reached Albany, my mother sat in the yellow chair, her afghan in a crumpled heap at her feet. "Daniel, explain to Grace. There is no reason for me to go to sleep before eleven. After my apple. You know that."

Grace tried to calm Mother. "Mary, if you stay up until eleven, you nap all day. Go to bed at nine. Then you enjoy the day."

My mother rejected the logic. "If I nap, I nap. That won't change, but I have to stay up until eleven."

I interceded: "Mother, Grace is concerned about you. Why do you want to stay up until eleven? Maybe we can work this out."

I knew the answer. Knew it before I asked. "Daniel, if I go to sleep at nine, how can I have an apple at eleven?"

Irrefutable logic. Even at eighty-nine my mother thought clearly and knew the enduring values of life.

"But, Mother, why don't you have an apple at nine? Look how fortunate you are. You have Grace. She has you. You like Macs. She likes Macs. Change your hour to nine o'clock. The Macs won't mind."

Silence. Mother reached for the afghan and covered her feet. She shook slightly.

"All right, Daniel. I'll do it. I'll go to bed at nine. But I don't want to. I don't want to. It's not the apples. It's just that nine comes too early. Nine comes too early."

A few months later, just shy of her ninetieth year, my mother died. And since that time I have often thought of her words: "Nine comes too early." Not to eat apples. You can eat apples at any hour, but for all those years the 11:00 P.M. apple hour signified a day fully lived. There would be enough time to sleep. The sleep of a single night. The sleep of eternity. And no matter what our age, 9:00 P.M. always comes too early. Especially the final 9:00 P.M. Yes, whether we are sixteen or forty, thirty-one or ninety-one, 9:00 P.M. comes too early. We are never ready to relinquish our hold on the waking hours, the promise of a new day. No matter what our age. So I savor the hours leading to 9:00 P.M. To 11:00 P.M. And I enjoy the apple, the single apple hanging from my tree on Tripp Street.

43. Reaping the Harvest

⎯⎯⎯⎯◎⎯⎯⎯⎯

Walt was a gentleman farmer specializing in tomatoes. A family man, Walt grew Small Fry tomatoes, Little Boys, Big Boys, Better Boys, Pink Girls, First Ladies. Tomato season commenced on Manure Day, when Harvey from the horse farm off Route 172 dropped his load of horse manure on Walt's tomato patch and Walt started planning for the coming spring.

For many years Walt gained peace of mind from tomato farming, but in his later years, as summer slowly burned itself out, Walt worried. "Soon winter will come and there are still green tomatoes on the plant. Will they turn red before winter plucks them from existence?" Walt had become the Man Who Had Empathy for Green Tomatoes. And on the night of a killer frost Walt shut himself in his house with the family Bible, read from the book of Job, and searched for the meaning of existence. "Why do bad winters happen to good tomatoes? Why? Why?"

Walt's obsession with tomatoes coincided with the time he was fitted for a hearing aid and forgot the name of his four-teenth grandchild, Celia's kid. As his depression deepened, Walt's family worried. But then in the spring of 1983 he bounced back, mobilized his energy, and mounted an attack on the green tomatoes—a battle described in the *Tripp Street Chronicles* under the chapter "Walt vs. the Forces of Nature." Details of Walt's strategy can be found on pages 39 to 107, but several examples should suffice.

The Tire Strategy. In mid-April as I walked by Walt's gar-den I noticed a row of tires to the right of the manure pile.

Walt called to me, "Well, what do you think, Dan?"

"Think?"

"About the tires."

I searched for an intelligent answer. "I think you have a classic, Walt. Probably from the artist's neo-rubber period. Did you buy it in a loft or in a flat? Have Mrs. Martha Parsons and the Tripp Street Garden Club reviewed the work?"

Walt wasn't amused. "Dan, these tires will give me a longer growing season. In April I can plant the tomatoes inside the tires. The sun will warm the rubber, the rubber will warm the tomato plants, and the fruit will redden earlier. Wait."

At first Walt seemed to be on to something. These toma-toes were going to have a Goodyear, and to show their appre-ciation they shot up faster than any tomatoes on the street. However, once they made it over the top, they resumed normal speed, and by frost the score remained Green tomatoes 17– Walt 0.

Was Walt discouraged? Certainly not. Inspired by a Yankee farmer who crossed a strawberry plant with milkweed and pro-duced strawberries and cream, Walt went south for the winter, determined to find another idea. The result?

Mountain Spring Tomatoes. In mid-September I received

Walt's Season's Greetings card, a picture of a beefsteak tomato with the caption "Great Tomatoes I Have Sown," and beneath the caption a message: "Save your Mountain Spring water jugs." In the spirit of community cooperation, everyone on Tripp Street drank Mountain Spring water. Old Luke gave up whiskey for Mountain Spring water, Marion switched from Diet Pepsi to Mountain Spring water, and in an act of solidarity Garth filled his swimming pool with Mountain Spring water. By the time of Walt's return his garden overflowed with Mountain Spring water jugs.

On planting day Walt set his tomatoes inside the tires, hammered stakes into the ground, and hung filled Mountain Spring water jugs from the stakes. "Solar heating," he explained. "The tires will warm the young plants, then the hot water takes over, and even when frost comes the water will store up heat and warm the tomatoes." We'll never know if his plan might have worked. On the night of the Big Frost the Mountain Spring water froze.

Hair Raising Tomatoes. This method of ripening tomatoes involved hair dryers. On the night of the Big Frost, Walt, his children, grandchildren, and great-grandchildren planned to convene in the garden and blow-dry the tomatoes until the morning sun. Before Walt left for Florida, Con Ed ran 500 feet of cable from Tripp Street out to his garden, and every store, from K Mart to Caldor, reported a run on hair dryers. With sadness I report that Walt did not live to execute this plan. He died at a ripe old age, leaving behind a legacy of tires, water jugs, hair dryers, and green tomatoes. As befitted Walt, the funeral was attended by all the residents of Tripp Street. His coffin, draped with tomato vines, captured the essence of the man, and the minister's words were both touching and appropriate:

"When we remember Walt may we remember the frailty of human nature, acknowledge that not one of us can hold back the onslaught of the Big Frost, influence the length of our days, or always reap the fullness of the harvest. Yes, my dear, dear friends, remember summer never lasts."

Tripp Street remembers, and on the eve of the Big Frost, officially designated as Green Tomato Day, we make a pilgrimage to Walt's resting place in the Eternal Garden Cemetery. There at the gravesite we place green tomatoes on his headstone and wish Walt well in his journey through the seasons.

44. Barry of the Butterflies

A lament for Barry.

Swoosh. Swoosh. Who is that man slimmer than a poplar, taller than a lilac, chasing through the meadow with a green net cutting the air? Barry the Butterfly Hunter! Swoosh. Swoosh. He has one. Black and orange. A six-inch wingspan. A Monarch. Barry B., who lives in the apartment above the stables, is Tripp Street's foremost butterfly collector. Swoosh. Swoosh. Barry drops the Monarch into a bottle, secures the lid, slips along the trail pursuing another prize.

Barry, once a science teacher in the Middle School, tracks butterflies, following them from furry caterpillar to cocoon to freedom to Barry's net. Swoosh. Swoosh. "Someday, Dan, I'll show you my books of butterflies, rare books."

"When, Barry, when?"

Barry smiles. "When I take them out of storage. My entire library, five thousand books, is in storage. They've been there since I moved to Tripp Street. Soon I will bring the books home. But not yet. Not yet."

Barry smiles. A sad smile framed by the white sun hat with the green band. Barry always wears the sun hat. On bright days. On gray days. In the fields. In his home. Dressed in khaki pants, a light blue windbreaker, and the hat, he searches for butterflies.

When I first met Barry he told me about the books packed in cartons, the closed volumes piled in the corner of Regan's Storage. And year after year he would lament, "If only I had my library. If only."

"Why not this year, Barry? Why not this year?"

And, as if in answer, Barry spreads the wings of the butterfly on a cardboard backing and turns away.

Barry collects butterflies. And he collects dreams.

"Dan, were you in Israel this summer?"

"Yes."

"Tell me again. The view from the Mount of Olives, overlooking the Golden Dome, the Temple Mount. How does it look in the early morning when the sun catches fire and the city flames in radiance?"

Barry speaks in poetry when he speaks of Israel. He has read every book on the Holy Land, from fourth-century pilgrims in search of God to twentieth-century archeologists in search of bedrock.

"Someday, Dan, you and I will visit the Promised Land. Tell me when you go again."

Each summer I invite Barry. Each summer he declines.

"This year my mother isn't well." "This year my apartment is being painted." "This year I promised to watch Lila's cat." "This year . . ." And the years pass.

When, Barry? When? You sit by the gates of your future waiting to enter the Promised Land. Waiting to move forward.

How long will you wait to fulfill your longing? Your life remains packed in storage. The years unfold, but you do not move with them. A time will come when it is too late to begin. Then what, Barry? Then what?

And Barry never answers, except with a smile rising to the brim of his sun hat. The white hat with the green band. Barry never answers. Instead he places a black and yellow butterfly between two panes of glass. Only hours before, the butterfly floated over daisies in the meadow. Now the Monarch hangs on a wall. Barry looks at the butterfly. All he sees is his own reflection captured in the glass.

45. Taconic Cider Mill

Over the river and through the woods,
To Taconic Cider Mill I go.
I don't know the way.
I don't have a sleigh . . .

The direct route to Taconic Cider Mill follows Route 142, but on this crisp October day I chose to walk the path through Bayberry Woods.

"Do you know where you're going?" Marion called after me.

Ever since I drove out of the garage on East Fifty-fifth Street headed for the East River Drive and found myself at the entrance to the West Side Highway, Marion has been leery of my sense of direction. On that occasion I explained, "Marion, with all the construction in New York City someone accidentally moved the West Side Highway to the East River and vice versa!" Marion was not convinced.

She also knows my family history. I am descended from a long line of mistake makers. For instance, when I was only a child living in Wilkes-Barre, Pennsylvania, our family went on an outing to Parsippany, New Jersey. (Who ever went to Parsippany, New Jersey, on a family outing?) Before leaving the house my mother asked, "Sam, do you have a map?" My father replied, "Now, dear, we're only going to Parsippany." Before you could spell Parsippany we were lost. Seeking redemption, my father followed a Cadillac. "Cadillacs always know their way," Dad explained. He was right. After we pursued the Cadillac for many hours, the big black car with the fancy fins pulled into a driveway on the outskirts of Baltimore, Maryland. The Cadillac lived in that driveway.

In spite of this genetic defect, who can lose his way in Bayberry Woods? I set out with confidence on paths covered with pine needles. Eventually a fork appeared. The right fork was marked by an empty Coca-Cola can, the left fork by a Snickers candy wrapper. After picking up the Snickers wrapper, I took that fork, only to find after several hours I was back at the Coca-Cola can. Lost. Walking in circles. Where was Taconic Cider Mill? Where was the East River Drive? Where was the West Side Highway? More important, where was I? It is bad enough not to know where you are going, it is even worse not to know where you are! The sun was overhead as I continued on into the depths of Bayberry Woods. Deeper. Deeper.

Then I heard the sound of footsteps. Twigs cracking. Had Marion sent Teddy after me? Good old Marion. Good old Teddy. But instead of Teddy a man appeared. A man of the forest, clothes woven from bark, a beard wild and unkempt, feet bound in rags. (In retrospect I believe the man wore a tweed sportcoat, but at the time I was delirious, needed a cider fix, and imagined a rugged woodsman.) Running toward my rescuer, I shouted, "Sir, I am lost. I've been walking for two hours. How do I get out of Bayberry Woods? Show me the path to Taconic Cider Mill."

The woodsman stared at me and his face erupted into a wry smile. "How long did you say you've been walking? Two hours? Well, my friend, I've been wandering since six this morning, over five hours. I wanted to be first on line at Taconic Cider Mill. I'm also lost. I even left a Snickers wrapper to mark the spot, but someone took the wrapper."

Returning the Snickers wrapper, I addressed my companion: "When I saw you I felt sure I was saved. You would lead me out of the woods. Now I see there is no hope."

"No hope?" he asked. "Look at it this way. We can't be found until we have been lost, and I've been lost since 6 A.M."

I shrugged. My companion was in worse shape than me. Just my luck to meet up with another loser. "So what's the point?"

"Isn't it something to admit you're on the wrong path? That's the first step in finding the right path. The path to Taconic Cider Mill."

And we were off.

46. The
Greyhound Bus

"Thin cars only!" If you're big and bulky, beware. Tripp Street is a narrow street. Very narrow, especially around the bend at the top of Murphy's Hill. Even in my car, a skinny little Toyota, I hold my breath, pull in my stomach, and pray the roadside hasn't wandered onto Tripp Street in the heavy spring rains. "Thin cars only!"

Last October a Greyhound bus, throwing caution to the exhaust, grunted and groaned up Murphy's Hill. Halfway up, the bus driver stuck his head out the window, flicked a Marlboro against the stone wall, and called to me, "Can I make it?"

"Nope! Not in a Greyhound. Come back tomorrow in a Thinny Thin car. Like a Toyota."

As the driver backed down the hill, more like a turtle than a greyhound, I noticed the sign above the front window. "Chartered: Foliage Tour"; one of those tour buses from New York City that poke around our neighborhood each fall in search of autumn leaves and historic houses. Clunk. Clunk. Clunk. The retreating Greyhound ran the maze of potholes and drove off in search of wider, fatter streets. In addition to a tailpipe, the touring Greyhound left behind a memory.

The year was 1964, several months after I had been ordained a rabbi.

The office phone rang. "Rabbi, we want to be married on June fourteenth. Are you free?" This was it. My first wedding. Unsolicited. They wanted me.

The caller, who introduced himself as Herman Hermanson, sounded quite mature. In fact, his voice sounded unnaturally old for a young man entering the blissful portals of matrimony. (I remembered that phrase from Practical Rabbinate 101.) Summoning my most clerical tone, I replied, "My good man, it will be the greatest of pleasures to consummate your marriage." (Later I learned "formalize" was more appropriate than "consummate.") "Come to my office at noon tomorrow for premarital counseling."

The next day Herman and Margaret entered my office, holding hands and a sprig of forsythia. Herman walked slowly, leaning on a cane, the last remaining strand of gray hair sticking out from a black hat. Margaret eased herself into a chair, gentle wrinkles lining a face still beautiful and softened by time.

Herman came right to the point: "Rabbi, I am ninety years old; my young bride only eighty-seven. I lost my beloved Sophie five years ago, and Margaret has been alone for seven years. Now we have found one another." Margaret gently stroked Herman's hand.

What do you say to a couple of octogenarians planning marriage? In my fifth year at the seminary I had taken Advanced Counseling 301: The Complexities of Baby-Naming Ceremonies (Should a family serve lox or whitefish?); Bar Mitzvahs (Are parents entitled to 50 percent of a child's monetary gifts?); Marriages (Should the couple say, "I do," "I will," or "Maybe"?); Retirement (Is Miami preferable to Arizona?); Death (Is it really over when it's over?). Unfortunately, Professor Blessings failed to cover premarital counseling for a couple with eleven great-grandchildren. I gave myself a pep talk. "Shape up, Rabbi. You can do it. Sure, you're unmarried and twenty-five, but you've been dating for eight years. You even took Samantha to the senior prom *and* the homecoming weekend. This is just a piece of cake. Wedding cake. Go out there and get 'em, Dan. Counsel!"

Fortunately, Herman and Margaret led me through the interview, and I acquired useful wisdom to carry down the aisles of future wedding ceremonies. When the hour ended, Herman leaned forward. "Rabbi, we have a request."

"Yes?"

He pulled a tarnished gold Elgin watch out of his watch pocket to emphasize a point. "Rabbi, Margaret and I want the wedding to be short. Either leave out a few prayers or read fast. Whatever you're comfortable with."

A reasonable request. I had unlimited time stretching before me (a mistaken conclusion held only by the young), but Herman and Margaret? Well, time was precious.

"Of course. Of course," I answered.

"I hope we didn't insult you, Rabbi, but the ceremony is set for three P.M. And at five we're leaving on our honeymoon. Have to catch the bus."

"Bus?"

"Yes, we're taking a ninety-nine-day Greyhound bus trip from New York to Los Angeles. Just Margaret and me. Holding hands all the way."

Margaret blushed beneath her white hair.

Suddenly a spark of inspiration kindled in my pastoral mind. I really could provide counsel to this couple. Help them understand their days were limited. If they wanted to reach the West Coast they should fly. Why waste ninety-nine days on a

Greyhound bus? I pulled a cherrywood pipe out of the pocket of my tweed jacket. (As a young rabbi I found a pipe added maturity to my image.) Lighting up, I sputtered, coughed, swallowed tobacco juice, grimaced, and pointed the pipe toward Herman and Margaret. Then with tact I suggested, "My beloved friends" (a common clergy expression I soon dropped), "why delay reaching the golden sands of the Pacific Coast traveling on a Greyhound? Fly. Fly. In five hours you can be in California riding the waves on a streamlined surfboard."

Margaret laughed. "I'm not sure we're of the age for surfboarding. That's for you, dear."

"Dear?" What had happened to my clerical cover? Drowned in a wave off Big Sur.

Herman smiled. "What's our hurry? Do you think we're too old to go driving off into the sunset?"

Choking on my pipe and pride, I blurted out, "But if you have someplace you want to go, shouldn't you get there as soon as possible? Isn't that true at any age?"

Margaret pulled her wool shawl around her neck, then spoke to me as she might have spoken to one of her grandchildren, or great-grandchildren.

"Rabbi, we've seen many places in these years that God's been good to us. Many places. But think of all the places we still have not seen, in Pennsylvania, Ohio, Wisconsin, Minnesota, Wyoming, Oregon. Why, between here and there a world waits to be explored. We would miss those places if we flew; miss all the points along the way. What a shame." Margaret stroked Herman's hand. A sparkle danced across Margaret's face, and played hide and seek with wrinkles engraved during her journey through the years. As they left my office holding hands and the sprig of forsythia, I realized that springtime is not only for the young.

I don't know what happened to Margaret and Herman Hermanson. Perhaps they are still bouncing along over the Dakota Badlands or winding down the coast of Monterey, stopping at every Greyhound station. And to the best of my knowledge, Greyhound has not returned to Tripp Street. But Greyhound occupies a special parking place in my memory. Greyhound and the Herman Hermansons, a reminder as I speed along the expressway of time to apply the brakes, enjoy the stations. And whenever a Greyhound bus passes I sneak a look inside. Who knows, maybe someday I'll see Margaret and Herman Hermanson nestled into their seats. Holding hands.

47. Danville, PA

~~~

Autumn. Apple cider at Taconic Cider Mill. Raking leaves. Trick-or-treating. A hayride. Jack-o'-lanterns. A harvest moon. The killer frost. Penn State football games. Most of all Penn State football games. Teddy and I curl up on the couch, turn on the television, nibble popcorn and dog bones, and watch Penn State football games. Why Penn State? I went to Brown. Teddy dropped out of dog-training school when in a pique of jealousy she bit a French poodle. So why Penn State? Free association. When I think of Penn State I think of Danville, PA, and when I think of Danville, PA, I think of Joseph Petrovsky, who added immeasurably to my higher education.

September 1960. The bus station in the sleepy town of Danville, PA, thirty miles from State Park, home of Penn State University, was empty except for a white-haired man leaning on a cane. "Rabbi?" he called. "Rabbi?" Was he speaking to me? Of course! I was a rabbinical student sent to Danville for the Jewish holy days. My charge? Preach, teach, inspire, console. I was twenty-one.

Mr. Owen Solomon shook my hand. "Rabbi, glad to have you in Danville. Real glad. But only fair to warn you. There won't be many people attending services this afternoon. Whoever chose today for our holy days made a real mess of it. Penn State's playing at home, and in these parts Penn State comes before God. Why, I've been president of this congregation for thirty-eight years, on the board fifty-three years, and I can tell you, if Penn State's playing at home, the only praying that's going on is for victory. Victory, Rabbi, victory. My suggestion to you, young man, when you get back to that seminary in Ohio, tell them to check their calendar with Penn State's football schedule. You people could avoid conflicts if the holy days stayed clear of State's home games. Don't mean to be presumptuous, Rabbi. Just a suggestion."

Mr. Owen Solomon called it as he saw it. As he had seen it for almost ninety-three years. A handful of people appeared for the afternoon memorial service. Solomon leaned my way during the silent prayer. "Everyone's really up for this service; just heard Penn State won by a point." On that note I read the names of congregants who had died during the past year. Rose Baker, Isaac Cohen, Robert Frankel, Mildred Solomon, Joseph Petrovsky. A murmur spread through the old wooden temple. In the far corner an elderly man sitting under a stained-glass Moses giggled.

I invoked God's blessing on Congregation House of Heaven (Penn State obviously did not need a blessing) and added a personal prayer of thanksgiving for surviving my first congregation. Then he approached. The man sitting under Moses.

"Rabbi, I want to thank you for reading my name."

I was puzzled. "Sir, when did I read your name?"

"Why, just now. You remembered me as one of those who

died during the past year. Joseph Petrovsky. And I wanted to thank you. No one ever reads my name at House of Heaven."

The color of my face matched the autumn maple shading the Temple. "S-s-sir. Mr. Petrovsky. I'm sorry. Oh, my God, what did I do? But your name was on the list. I'm sure."

I looked closely at the list. "We wish to thank Joseph Petrovsky for donating the pulpit flowers."

I felt as if I had just been tackled by the entire Penn State football team.

Petrovsky shrugged. "Since I seem to have died this year, perhaps you could tell me what you said in my eulogy."

Petrovsky was letting me off the ground.

"Well, of course, sir. I only give praise in a eulogy! Have you ever heard anyone defame a person in their eulogy? I'm sure I spoke about your devotion to your family, the little ones who called you Pop-Pop, beloved of those who knew you, respected in business, highest ethical standards . . ."

Petrovsky beamed. "Splendid, Rabbi, splendid. You're just beginning in the religion business, but you're off to a fine start. Simply fine. I wonder if you'd come home with me, meet my daughter and her husband. They apologize for not being here, but you could hardly expect them to give up their seats on the fifty-yard line. Anyway, I want you to tell them you read my name as one of those who died during the past year. They'll get a kick out of that! Then I want you to repeat the eulogy you just gave. Flesh it out a bit while we're driving home, but keep it under five minutes. Will you do that for me?"

At that moment I contemplated taking early retirement from the clergy. Twenty-one seemed like a ripe old age to consider a second career. But Joseph Petrovsky's eyes burned to the very depths of my robe and I couldn't walk away.

"Sir, why do you want me to repeat the eulogy? The entire incident was a mistake. I'm sorry, but couldn't we just keep this our own little secret?"

"A secret? Nonsense. By now, Rabbi, all Danville knows I

left this world. And you want to keep the eulogy a secret? A mistake. A grave mistake (sorry for the pun). Too many of us keep eulogies secret until after a person dies. Hold off saying all the good things. Then we overflow with praise. In life we criticize. In death we praise. My daughter, for instance. We're close. Very close. But when I consider how often she criticizes me. How often I criticize her. Seems to me I should gather up all the love, respect, satisfaction I feel for my family and my friends. Gather it up in a huge wooden barrel. Then each autumn I'll take the lid off the barrel and share the harvest."

Petrovsky grinned. "Didn't mean to preach to a rabbi. Let's just say I'd like to hear them praise me while I'm still around, before the whistle blows and the game is over. Think about it, Rabbi."

So I thought about it and in my course on the Practical Ministry shocked the seminary with two radical proposals: 1) Don't wait until it's too late to praise the ones you love. 2) Check the Penn State football schedule before fixing the dates of the holy days.

. . .

I don't know whether anybody listened, but every fall as Teddy and I watch a Penn State football game, I hope they did. I sure hope they did.

48. Jason Chases the Moon

———⟲———

Why did Jason and I set out to catch the moon?

On a clear night when the moon rises over Murphy's Hill, you can see ivy vines climb the stone stable and glisten with magic. The chimneys of Otto's home pierce the air. Deer silhouetted in the fields gaze at passersby, and the pavement shimmers with moonrays sneaking through the pine trees. But on black moonless nights I collide with telephone poles, trip in potholes, and sink into the puddle across from Lila's house. That's why I set out to catch the moon. If I had the moon, then even the darkest nights would shine like daytime.

My plan called for a partner. After talking to several neighbors who considered me eccentric—"Sure, Dan, sure, you can store the moon in our garage"—I realized my idea needed the innocence of youth. Jason. My partner in butterfly hunting and boomerang throwing. Jason. A little boy who dreamed and who was on a first-name basis with E.T., Luke Skywalker, and other extraterrestrial beings. Jason and me. Moonshiners Incorporated.

I explained the scheme to Jason. "Jason, we are very lucky to live on Tripp Street."

"Why?"

"Because when the moon visits earth it lands on Tripp Street."

Jason's eyes filled with stars. "Where does it land? Please, let me know!"

"Well, Jason, on a moonlit night the moon comes into your backyard and lies in the pond where you fish."

"Heron Pond?"

"Exactly! On a sparkling night when the moon rises over the pond you can see the same moon in the water. Near the shore. And we can catch it! I know we can!"

Jason was so excited that he blew a bubble with his bubble gum. First time he had ever blown a bubble. A big round sticky yellow bubble. Like the moon.

"Tonight, Jason, bundle up and meet me in your backyard. At the pond. Next to the tree stump where we first saw the heron."

At 8:30 on an October night, Jason quietly eased his way out the back door while the babysitter and her boyfriend watched *Raiders of the Lost Ark* on the VCR. I hesitated. Was it wrong taking little Jason out of his house at 8:30 on a school night? But once we came home dragging the moon, everyone would understand. Anyway it was too late. Jason was out the door, wearing a blue parka and jeans.

"Jason, first we have to unroll this chicken wire. Careful. Don't prick yourself. Now, carry the wire to the edge of the pond. See, as the moon climbs higher into the sky it creeps along the water. When it comes here I'll wade into the pond and we will make a fence around the moon. Then we will have the moon!"

Jason let out a yelp of pleasure. "Shh, Jason. You will frighten the moon away."

When the moonlight was several feet from the shoreline, I put the plan into action. Slipping on swamp cabbage, I almost fell into the moon but regained my footing. Encircling the yellow ball of light with wire fencing, I cried out, "Gotcha! Gotcha! Gotcha! Gotcha!" the special word I had stored up for this moment. Then Jason and I laid transparent plastic over the moon cage, bound the plastic with ties from a box of Hefty garbage bags, and stood back to admire our work. Overhead a meteor shower shot shooting stars across the sky. "Heavenly applause," I explained to Jason. "Tomorrow morning, before school, we will place the moon in my Toyota wagon. Now, run on home."

Well, you know the rest of the story. Next morning the moon was nowhere to be seen. Vanished into thin air. Jason and I searched under rocks, behind stone walls, even under Otto's Mercedes, but somehow the moon had escaped. In the evening I went to comfort Jason. It was a dark evening, and I bumped into a Volkswagen, stubbed my toe on a tree, and inched my way along Tripp Street.

"What happened?" Jason asked. "Who took our moon?"

"I'm not sure, Jason. We should have put an alarm system on the fence. Next time."

"Can we try again tonight? Please? Maybe we can do something else."

How could I explain to an eight-year-old that the moon will always elude our grasp? He'll learn soon enough that life is not meant to be lighted all the way. We can never eliminate dark nights. And heaven tinkering? A risky occupation. But I didn't want to discourage the boy. At any age we should try to brighten our path. Try. Even if we fail. Far worse than failing is not trying.

"Sorry, Jason, tonight I have a meeting. But don't worry, one of these nights I'll be back. And if I'm not here, go out there on your own. And think of me."

49. The Heron

~~⊚~~

Maps of Westchester County omit Heron Pond. The pond I named. Heron Pond is easy to find. Encompassed by a rock ridge and pine trees, Heron Pond stands at the summit of Murphy's Hill. Most people familiar with Tripp Street consider my pond an overgrown puddle. Perhaps they are correct. Heron Pond extends approximately a hundred feet by thirty feet, and even frogs spurn Heron Pond for more impressive croaking grounds. Still, Heron Pond falls within Noah Webster's definition of a pond: "a body of water usually smaller than a lake." Much smaller.

When did Heron Pond receive her name? The Indian summer day when a heron visited Tripp Street. On that late October day a gaggle of geese deserting the north flew south. As the last geese disappeared, I saw the heron serenely poised on a tree stump offshore. Propped on his long legs, gray head scanning the pond, the heron was the first I had ever seen on Tripp Street. Unfortunately, the bird didn't realize we are a friendly street, and as Cal's Jeep drove by he craned his neck and rose in fright. With a flapping of giant wings, the heron soared into the heavens, silhouetted against the blue sky.

When the heron flew away I realized I had been witness to one of those precious moments we hope will last forever. They never do. But the following day the heron reappeared, circling, circling overhead, lost in a grove of pine boughs, then descending gracefully onto the tree stump. This time I grabbed my camera and whispered to the heron, "Wait! Don't move! Don't leave! Face me. That's it, pirouette to the left. Perfect!" I focused on the heron's head, tucked into the crook of its neck. The sharp outline of silver feathers reflected in the lens. I pressed the shutter. The sound frightened the heron. What did he know of camera shutters, my visitor from the Adirondack Mountains, raised with the echo of a snapping twig, a chipmunk scurrying under a blanket of leaves, a trout breaking water? What did he know of the voice of civilization? Once more the heron rose above the rock cliff and followed a trail of cotton-candy clouds into the distant sky.

Both Indian summer and the heron left Heron Pond, traveling a distant path. "Don't leave!" I had pleaded on that October day. But the heron vanished, flying on a zephyr of the wind. Further, further from my view. I knew then, and I know now, all of life, all we love, eventually departs, leaving our voice to flutter in the wind. The seasons pass. Forever. Winter comes.

The pond lies empty. But the photograph remains of a heron hovering above a pond on Tripp Street. And that photograph stirs memory. Once again the heron comes to Heron Pond, caresses the lonely heart, and reawakens moments never lost. If we remember.

50. Autumn Leaves

At witches' time, when magic creatures glide in on cornhusk brooms, I stretch out on the stone wall and watch leaves flutter to the ground. Flaming reds and gold and auburn. When I was still a child my father would search for fallen leaves under the forsythia and beneath the mountain ash, the prongs of his metal rake gathering the last traces of summer in giant piles, higher than a boy of seven. When I was still a child. Then I would leap from pile to pile, down, down, into myriad dry leaves, and a season would pass. Even now, many seasons later, I smell the smoke of burning leaves or imagine black and gray spirals rising above the trees as the leaves return to a distant home. Nostalgia floats in every corner of the sky, and sadness fills the air.

Autumn is a time of loss. Why must the radiant leaves of autumn fall from their branches? Why do gusts of wind shake

out the patchwork quilt covering the world? The scientist answers: "In autumn the chlorophyll parts from the leaf, taking
with it the vibrant green. Then the leaf turns and falls." I do
not doubt the wisdom of the scientist, but there is another
explanation, as there always is, of the mysteries of the universe,
an explanation better suited to the glory of autumn.

According to legend, in the days before rakes, perhaps even
the days before witches, the leaves were summoned before their
creator. "Your days are numbered. Prepare for flight." When
the leaves heard this message they raised a wisp of protest. "Our
days are too brief. Why must we fall to earth? Why? Why?"
And of course the leaves had a point. Even the baseball season
lasts longer than the time allotted leaves on trees.

But the decree was irrevocable. Gently their creator explained. "I understand. Through the summer you go out on a
limb to shade the earth, provide nesting sites for birds, fill the
air with the rustle of your music. And who would wish to part
from a majestic tree? I understand. But soon winter will arrive,
and the ground, barren and unprotected, will lie forsaken. Except for you. You will cover the earth. That is why you fall. To
warm the ground when snow falls. As you had a purpose in
spring and summer, so your journey in autumn will serve the
world in winter. And when blizzards swirl, the earth will praise
you. Don't you understand?"

The leaves understood, but still they were sad. Seeing their
anguish, the creator made a promise. "Before you fall I will be-
stow upon you the gift of color. Reds and pinks, yellow to catch
the light. And auburn, yes, auburn will grace your surface."

As it was promised, it happened. The sun illuminated the
autumn leaves. And who can forget their colors? They remain
with us throughout the winter days.

One phase of life always ends before another can begin. But
brilliant colors never vanish. Colors of leaves, of love, of life,
linger despite loss, casting the warmest tones upon the coldest
days. Covering the heart of the bereaved.

51. Hand in Hand

What is middle age? Halfway between Miss Abercrombie's and the Homestead.

. . .

"Nicky," I heard Amy say as she walked down Tripp Street with her son. "Nicky, tomorrow you will begin Little Chickadee Nursery School, then law school, and someday you will have children of your own."

Were those the words my mother said in 1942? Hand in hand we were walking along River Street headed for my first day in Miss Abercrombie's Nursery School. Mother was not speaking of law school. She was reminding me: "You're lucky, Daniel. Lucky. After biting Miss Abercrombie in the interview, I'm surprised she accepted you; and after we said you were toilet-trained and relate well to others. You're lucky." Lucky? To have to go to nursery school? Lucky? Well, too late. We were already at the gate, and Miss Abercrombie, all two hundred pounds of her, had swept me up in her arms. "Daniel, we'll have so much fun together." Fun? To this day I do not know why I believed Miss Abercrombie. (For the record: I trace my eventual loss of faith back to Miss Abercrombie and that meeting by the sandbox.) As Miss Abercrombie gurgled and bubbled, I clung to Mother's hand and watched pigtailed girls swing on creaky wooden swings. Miss Abercrombie urged me to play ring-around-the-rosy with Susie, Bethy, and Bobby. Mother let go of my hand.

Details are a bit fuzzy at this point, but according to family history I bolted for the fence. If the wire had not caught my navy blue shorts, I would have been over and out. Instead, Mother intercepted the Ascension of Daniel and promised Miss Abercrombie I would adjust. After several days of hand holding I did adjust, and by year's end had collected more than my share of gold stars, which my mother framed. They hang next to the honorary doctorate I received in 1988.

The memory of my mother's hand and Miss Abercrombie surfaced several years ago as I drove along a country road covered with flowing red leaves, the last burst of the passing season. My mother sat next to me. She was almost ninety. Our destination was an adult residence, the old stone estate known as the Homestead. Mother was recuperating from a series of strokes and a hospital stay. In the hospital she had said, "Daniel, the last time I was in the hospital was forty-eight years ago when you were born. Then I left the hospital with a special gift. Now I don't know what I will leave with." Her fears were well founded. She left disoriented, anxious, and we hoped the move to the Homestead would give comfort.

Mrs. Evans, administrator at the Homestead, had assured me that my mother would receive loving care. "It's the best decision you could make." The best or the least worse? Mrs.

Evans continued: "I trust your mother will adjust, but if for some reason she does not, if she wanders or can't relate to the other women, well . . . we will need to reconsider." Even at this stage it was necessary to play ring-around-the-rosy.

With heavy heart, I parked outside the home, where women in their eighties and nineties relaxed on a stone patio. A tabby cat made the rounds, softly rubbing against one leg, then another. Mother and I began the climb up a flight of stone steps. She took my hand and tightened her grip. "You know, Daniel, the older I become, the higher the steps become." On the third step she stopped. Her pink dress hung loosely on her tiny frame as she smoothed several wisps of white hair and sighed. "I hope I look put together." We rested. Squeezing my hand, she climbed higher until we reached the stone arches marking the entrance to the Homestead. "Daniel." Her voice caressed the November day as she looked at our hands inter-twined. "Daniel, do you remember when you were young I took your hand? Now you take mine. We've come full cycle. Do you remember?"

I looked at the frail woman who had once taken me to Miss Abercombie's Nursery School and I answered, "Yes, Mother, I remember."

52. Will Day

"**Y**our presence is requested at the home of Walter B. Casper on Will Day, November 19, 10:30 A.M. Frederick E. Calloway Esq."

Will Day? Who added Will Day to the Tripp Street calendar? Flipping to November 19, I noted a single entry: "173 More Shopping Days to Jason's Birthday." Not a word concerning Will Day. Our calendar was established in the year 1 A.D. "After Domino's" (1981, the year after Domino's Pizza opened in town). Since that time street approval was necessary before a new day could be added to the calendar. Strict standards applied. For instance, the Tripp Street Pothole Association decided whether or not the pavement could bear the strain of another celebration. And Artichokes Anonymous, our garden club, debated nature holidays. Old Luke, quoting from Very

Very Old Luke, decided if the observance had traditional merit.
Now along came Frederick E. Calloway Esq., not even a resident of Tripp Street, and poof, "by the power invested in me"
had joined Tripp Street to Will Day. The nerve!

On November 19 I threaded my way through Walt's overgrown garden, still littered with tins and water jugs from his
tomato experiments, and entered the stone house. Walt's family and a delegation of neighbors had assembled in the library,
where oak shelves held volumes of *Organic Gardening* magazines
and an assortment of Walt's knickknacks—an empty DDT can,
the wheel of Walt's first wheelbarrow, two feet of cracked green
hose, and a Stormin' Norman Rockwell watercolor entitled
"Young Grubs at Play in the Garden."

Walt's family from the Midwest had arrived the night before, and Lydia, Max, Otto, and Old Luke were there from
Tripp Street. At precisely 10:30 A.M. Frederick E. Calloway
Esq. stuck his gold watch back into the watch pocket of his
brown vest, cleared his throat, and faced the gathering. "Thank
you for coming to Will Day, where we reveal the last wishes of
your relative and friend Walter B. Casper." And with that,
Frederick E. Calloway Esq. opened his leather briefcase and
read from the last will and testament of Walter B. Casper. "My
dear family, I have asked you to be here at this final moment as
a gesture of family closeness and solidarity." Off in one corner
a woman in her mid-twenties dressed in black slacks leaned
over to her father and asked, "Who is that elderly lady with the
pink hair? See, over there next to the bald man with the pipe."

"Dear, that's your Aunt Genevieve and Uncle Rudolf.
Don't you remember? They came to your fifth birthday party.
The party when Jiggs the Monkey roller-skated down the drive-
way."

The daughter smiled. "I remember Jiggs. But Aunt Genevieve and Uncle Rudolf?"

The lawyer continued reading from Walt's will. "In addition to my family I have asked those neighbors who were with

me at my coming in to also be with me at my going out." Otto wiped away the tears as he thought back to the summer day in 1979 when Walt came into Tripp Street and renovated the old horse stables, replacing the signs in the stalls—Citation, High Jumper, and Plows Ahead—with the names of his children, Karen, Jessica, and Jared.

Frederick E. Calloway's voice droned on.

"My set of sterling silver flatware, consisting of three demitasse spoons, one butter knife, and a fork, I leave to my niece Matilda of Dubuque, Iowa." Matilda was touched.

Since a will remains the last opportunity to instruct those who remain, Walt's bequest to his brother, George, included a word of explanation. "To George, I leave my wardrobe. Although I weigh a mere 120 pounds and George weighs in at 285 pounds, I trust the opportunity to wear my red and green plaid slacks will convince George to diet." Brother George gagged on the cream puff stuck in his mouth.

"And lest I forget the young ones, I leave my grandson Barney my set of baseball cards, consisting of one Mickey Mantle, one Pete Rose, one Shoeless Joe Jackson, and one Kevin Costner. In addition I leave Barney my three barely chewed pieces of bubble gum from a 1956 package of Topps Baseball Cards."

A hush filled the library. George stopped munching on his cream puff, Barney blew one bubble and fastened his gum to the fireplace mantel, and Matilda, still moved by the three demitasse spoons, stifled her sniffling. Frederick E. Calloway Esq. leaned over to a card table and lifted Walt's prized possessions, a porcelain panda and a porcelain penguin. The room erupted. "Walt promised the porcelains to me," a shrill voice from Cedar Rapids called out.

"Liar!" George called out. "Walt and I won Panda and Penguin when we were together in Atlantic City. They're mine!"

Even sweet niece Matilda entered the fray. "I'll trade one

demitasse spoon and a butter knife for the pair." When the family shouted down Matilda, she picked up the sterling silver butter knife, and if Barney hadn't retrieved his bubble gum and stuck it on Matilda's dagger hand, tragedy might have ensued. Fortunately, Walt, aware of possible dissension, had written, "I wish I could take the porcelains with me. Not that I'll have much use for them where I'm going, but I am afraid they could threaten family harmony. Therefore I am leaving Penguin and Panda to the Bronx Zoo to dispose of as they may deem proper."

The remainder of the will proceeded without incident. "To Old Luke I leave my old Sears catalog. To Lydia (dentist in residence) I leave my rake with the two missing teeth. To Dan I leave the trowel."

I trudged home disappointed, hoping to receive Walt's spade. Instead he left the spade to the First Methodist Church for their annual garden raffle. Slumping into the yellow wing chair, I reflected on the events of Will Day. At the end of my days, what would I bequeath? Walt's trowel, once removed? or would the trowel have rusted into oblivion? What remains of real worth to leave to another generation?

Then my thoughts wandered to another reading of a will. The year was 1957, the year my father died. My mother and I had gathered in the lawyer's chambers in Albany, New York, to hear my father's last will and testament. He left few material possessions; nothing to divide among aunts and uncles, nothing to argue over.

His will stated, "I am in possession of a far richer store. It is a way of life transmitted to me through thousands of years by prophet, sage, and martyr of my people. It embodies a counsel for life which, if taken diligently to heart and practiced by all men, would lead to larger understanding, less bloodshed, and more brotherhood. It is a counsel which thinks of man as a little lower than the angels rather than as kin to the beasts. That counsel I gladly bequeath to all mankind, without regard to family ties or color or creed. It is a rich heritage which, without distinction, I will to friend and foe alike."

Dad did not bequeath a single demitasse spoon or a Mickey Mantle baseball card. (Although he would have admired Mickey Mantle.) He did not even leave a porcelain panda or penguin. But he left a counsel, a set of values based on respect, understanding, the dignity inherent in every man and every woman. And the more he gave, the more he had to give. My father passed on few worldly possessions, but he bequeathed an understanding of the enduring worth of Matilda, George, Barney, and all of God's creatures. A legacy bequeathed to everyone.

"In witness whereof, I have hereunto set my hand and seal this 14th day of March, in the year one thousand nine hundred and fifty-six. Samuel Wolk. L.S."

What will you leave behind?